# Reference Interviews, Questions, and Materials

## Second Edition

edited by
THOMAS P. SLAVENS

The Scarecrow Press, Inc.
Metuchen, N.J., & London
1985

**Library of Congress Cataloging in Publication Data**

Slavens, Thomas P., 1928-
  Reference interviews, questions, and materials.

  Rev. ed. of: Informational interviews and questions /
edited by Thomas P. Slavens.  1978.
  1. Reference services (Libraries)  2. Reference
books.  3. College students--Library orientation.
4. Bibliography--Methodology--Study and teaching
(Higher)  I. Slavens, Thomas P., 1928-      .  Informational
interviews and questions.  II. Title.
Z711.S6  1985           028.7       85-1968
ISBN 0-8108-1797-7

Original edition entitled Informational Interviews and Questions

To Cora

# TABLE OF CONTENTS

# PREFACE

The purpose of this book is to assist students in learning to use reference materials. It is based on the idea that the best way to learn to use these works is to use them. It is intended for library science students in their first course in reference materials and for students in colleges and secondary schools for library orientation and bibliographical instruction programs.

The book is divided into chapters based on types of reference works: encyclopedias, yearbooks, statistical sources, biographical works, bibliographies and library science reference works, dictionaries, handbooks, serial publications, directories, and government publications. Within these chapters, three subdivisions are provided. The first of these subdivisions is labeled "Reference Interviews." These conversations are stenographically recorded interviews which have taken place in public, academic, school, and special libraries. Permission has been secured from the libraries involved to do this task, which required 700 hours to accomplish. At the same time, it is impossible to identify any patron or librarian involved in this project.

The reason for including these interviews is to give students some idea of the real world in which they will be working. None of the interviews has been created artificially. It would be useful for students of library science to attempt to answer these questions to give them a sense of realistic questions which are asked in libraries, as well as to understand how such questions are frequently phrased and the degree of skill which is required to elicit from patrons the exact nature of the information desired.

The second subdivision in each chapter is a list of reference questions which can be answered from basic reference sources. The reason for including these is the belief that the student wanting to know how to use reference materials can attend lectures and discussion groups on reference books; but until they use the works to locate data, they do not understand fully the types of materials available to meet the informational needs of readers.

A third subdivision in each chapter is a list of reference books in which the answers to the questions may be located.

An answer key to all the questions in the book will be supplied to teachers requesting such a key, addressed to the publisher on official stationery. Every attempt will be made, however, to safeguard the security of these answers.

Each professor will have to determine how many of these questions are to be used. One of the reasons for including so many is that the questions can be divided among students, thus reducing the probabilities of collaboration in answering them--if a teacher finds this undesirable.

In short, then, this book is intended to be useful to students as they attempt to become acquainted with a wide spectrum of representative sources of information and to learn to use these in meeting the informational needs of readers. For library orientation programs, it is hoped that the book will be useful in acquainting students with the wide variety of general reference materials available.

Finally, acknowledgment must be given to Professor Emeritus Raymond L. Kilgour of the School of Library Science at the University of Michigan. He was a master teacher of reference, who "willed" to the author some of the questions included in the book, although a great many have been added to this inheritance. The cooperation of the librarians who participated in the preparation of the book is acknowledged, although this group is so large that it would be impossible to name them all. Mention must be made, however, of three research assistants, Janice McIlwain, Alicia Palma-Lesko, and Charles Ten Brink.

Thomas P. Slavens
Professor of Library Science
The University of Michigan

# CHAPTER 1

## ENCYCLOPEDIAS

### Reference Interviews

Patron #1.    A woman caller

Patron:       What can you tell me about New Britain, Con-
              necticut?
Librarian:    Do you want to know where it's located or what
              it contains?
Patron:       I want information like what industries are
              there, and if there are any colleges or univer-
              sities there.

              Where would you look?


Patron #2.    A high school boy.

Patron:       I was wondering if you could help me find a list
              of all the Roman emperors?
Librarian:    Do you just want a list or some information on
              them?
Patron:       Just a list.

              Where could a list be found?


Patron #3.    A high school boy.

Patron:       Do you have a history encyclopedia?
Librarian:    What was it that you had in mind to look up?

Patron:      I need a chapter on the Gold Rush.
Librarian:   In the United States?
Patron:      Yes.
Librarian:   Do you know when it happened?  There were
             several, I think.
Patron:      The one I want was around 1848.
Librarian:   Is there any other word we could use for Gold
             Rush?
Patron:      Sometimes they're called the Forty-Niners.

Where would you find this information?


Patron #4.   An elementary school boy.

Patron:      We're studying maps.   Where can I find infor-
             mation on them?
Librarian:   Are you studying history or kinds of maps or
             something else?
Patron:      Kinds of maps.
Librarian:   Did you want books, magazine articles, or en-
             cyclopedia articles?
Patron:      I just want something I can read here.

What would you suggest?


Patron #5.   A high school boy.

Patron:      Does the library have a pamphlet on fascism?
Librarian:   Are you doing a report for school?
Patron:      Yes.
Librarian:   Just fascism in general or some more specific
             aspect of it?
Patron:      Just in general.
Librarian:   Did you check the card catalog for a book?
Patron:      Yes, but I don't want to read a book.

Where could you find general information?


Patron #6.   A junior high school boy.

Patron:      We're studying languages in school.   Where do
             I go to find out about them?
Librarian:   Do you have any special language in mind?
Patron:      Yes, I'm supposed to find out about pidgin English.

Where could you check?

---

Patron #7.  A man.

Patron:        Do you have a picture of the Colossus of
               Rhodes?
Librarian:     Is that one of the Seven Wonders of the World?
Patron:        Yes.  It was a statue but I think it's been torn
               down now.

               Where could sketches be found?

---

Patron #8.  An elementary school boy.

Patron:        My teacher said to find out about this.  (He
               hands the reference librarian a note with the
               word "equus" printed on it. )
Librarian:     Do you know anything about this equus at all?
Patron:        No.
Librarian:     What are you studying in class?
Patron:        Horses.
Librarian:     Do you think maybe this is a kind of horse?
Patron:        It could be.

               Where would you find this information?

---

Patron #9.  A high school boy.

Patron:        Where do I find information on the Ku Klux
               Klan?  It's not listed in the Readers' Guide.
Librarian:     That seems odd.  How are you spelling it?
Patron:        Cu Cluck Clan.
Librarian:     It's spelled with k's and the middle word is
               Klux.
Patron:        Oh, I'll check again.
Librarian:     Most of those articles are about recent events.
               Did you want an historical look at the Klan; for
               instance, what its role was following the Civil
               War?
Patron:        Yes, that was my assignment.

               Where would you locate this information?

Patron #10. A student.

| | |
|---|---|
| Patron: | I want some information on meiosis. |
| Librarian: | For which class is this? |
| Patron: | Biology. |
| Librarian: | Do you have to write a report? |
| Patron: | Yes, and I want to make a chart. |

Where would you look?


Patron #11. An elementary school boy.

| | |
|---|---|
| Patron: | I need to find out all about Michigan's forests. |
| Librarian: | Do you want to find out where they are located, how to be a forester, or Michigan's forests as an industry? |
| Patron: | I need to know about where they are and what kinds of trees they have and stuff. |

Where could you check first?


Patron #12. An elementary school boy.

| | |
|---|---|
| Patron: | Do you have any books about costumes? |
| Librarian: | Yes we do.  Do you want a book on how to make costumes or costumes of different countries and times? |
| Patron: | Well, I really want pictures of army uniforms. |
| Librarian: | Oh, I see.  Do you want foreign army uniforms or American ones? |
| Patron: | Well, sort of.  I have to do a project in school about the Revolutionary War.  We can do anything we want so I thought I'd draw pictures of the different uniforms of the Revolutionary War soldiers. |

Where would you look for good illustrations?


Patron #13. A man.

| | |
|---|---|
| Patron: | Say, I've got a problem.  Do you know anything about potatoes? |
| Librarian: | What do you want to know about potatoes?  How to grow them?  How to cook them? |

Patron:        Oh no, nothing like that.  You see, a few guys
               at work have a bet going.  One guy says that
               sweet potatoes and yams are the same thing, and
               the rest of us say that there's a difference.  Can
               you find out for me?

               Where would you check?


Patron #14.  A high school boy.

Patron:        Do you have any books about tobacco?
Librarian:     We have several books on smoking and also botany
               books which would contain information on tobacco.
               What exactly are you looking for?
Patron:        Well, I'm doing a paper on smoking and its his-
               tory and I want to find out who discovered to-
               bacco and where it's grown, how they make it
               into cigarettes and cigars and stuff like that.

               Where could you locate this information?


Patron #15.  A student.

Patron:        I need some information about Iwo Jima, you
               know, the mountain where they put up the flag.
Librarian:     Do you know the name of the mountain?
Patron:        It is Mt. Suribachi.
Librarian:     I don't see anything under Iwo Jima or Mt. Suri-
               bachi.  The entry must be World War II.

               Where would you look?


Patron #16.  A student.

Patron:        I need to find out about Christianity.
Librarian:     Is this for history class?
Patron:        Yes.
Librarian:     That is a big subject.  What phase of it do you
               need?
Patron:        I don't know.  Just general, I guess.

               Where could you find general information?


Patron #17.  A student.

Patron:        I want some information on Gutenberg.
Librarian:     Is this for your Bible class?
Patron:        No, it is for English composition class.
Librarian:     Do you need mostly information on the Gutenberg
               Bible or on Johann Gutenberg?
Patron:        I have to give an oral report on some of the
               characteristics of Gutenberg; a character sketch.

               Where could this be found?


Patron #18. A student.

Patron:        I want to find a copy of the text of the 25th Amend-
               ment to the Constitution.
               Where would you check?


Patron #19. A small girl.

Patron:        Do you have any books about cows?
Librarian:     What kind of book did you want?   A picture book
               or a story book?
Patron:        Well, I want to know if a cow has two stomachs
               or not.

               Where could this be answered?


Patron #20. A student.

Patron:        Do you have any books on the 13 colonies?
Librarian:     We have a section of books on early American
               history.
Patron:        I have a list of questions on who founded the
               colonies, etc.
Librarian:     The Oxford Companion to American History gives
               names and dates of ratification.
Patron:        I need more information than that.   I have six
               questions on various things.

               What would you suggest?

## Reference Questions

1.  Compare the bibliography for the article, "Acts of the
    Apostles" in the EB and the EA.  Which has the longer
    article?

2.  Compare closely the biographical detail given in the EB
    and the EA for Louis Agassiz, 1807-1873.

3.  What is the meaning of "Aijeleth Shahar"?

4.  Compare the anatomical illustrations in EA and Grand
    Larousse, e. g. , eyes, muscles, etc.  Which are better?

5.  Find a table showing the illegitimate children of
    Louis Quatorze.

6.  What work by Aristophanes did Frank Kupka, 1871-1957,
    illustrate?

7.  Find a portrait facsimile of Sir Richard Arkwright,
    famous British inventor.

8.  Who was responsible for the posthumous publication
    and popularity of the writings of Gustavo Adolfo Béc-
    quer?  Was there an English translation before the 20th
    century?

9.  Compare the entries on "Birds" in the WB and Comp-
    ton's.  Which do you think is better?

10. Find a portrait of Nicholas Murray Butler (1862-1947).

11. Locate a brief sketch of Maria Callas.

12. Where would you find color illustrations of Carolingian
    art?

13. Which has the better maps and illustrations for China,
    Compton's or the World Book?

14. Compare the costume illustrations of the Grand Larousse
    with those under "Clothing" in the World Book.

15. Name some of the superior characteristics of hybrid
    corns over other varieties.

16.   Can you find a picture of the 14th Dalai Lama of Tibet?

17.   Wanted:  pictures of some of the work by the famous
      sculptor Enrique Claraso y Daudi.

18.   Find an illustration of Jacque-Louis David's painting of
      Madame Récamier.

19.   Where is "S. Agnese" by Andrea del Sarto?   Locate
      a reproduction.

20.   Find a map of the city of Dessau.

21.   Find an illustration of a bust of Titus Flavius Domitian,
      Roman emperor.

22.   Locate a brief illustrated sketch on ancient Egyptian
      funeral architecture.

23.   When and where is the Feast of Dolls celebrated?

24.   Find the music (13 bars) of the national hymn of Fin-
      land.

25.   What is the English translation of the refrain of the
      French national anthem?

26.   Locate a statement of Gadow's classification of birds
      which includes a list of the principal characteristics
      of each category.

27.   Find articles on Alexandre Gendebien.

28.   Wanted:  an article in English which will give one a
      scholarly, historical treatment of genealogy.

29.   To which encyclopedia would you go for a disposition
      of the opposing forces at Gettysburg; and to which for
      a clear plan of the battle area; and to which for illus-
      trations?

30.   Where is the Gogebic Range located?

31.   When was gold first discovered in California, and by
      whom?

32.   Where may be found a reproduction in color of a page
      from the Gutenberg 42-line Bible?

33. Find illustrations of the Houyhnhnms and the inhabitants of Laputa.

34. Find a table showing the changes--name and territorial-- made in the states of India since 1947.

35. Find a list of notable persons, with dates, whose homes were or are in Iowa--a list containing at least 25 names.

36. Did Isyllus of Epidaurus dedicate a poem to Apollo of Malea?

37. Who sculpted the Iwo Jima Memorial, Arlington, Virginia? When was it dedicated?

38. What was the size of the army allowed to Jehoahaz by Hazael?

39. Where and when was the composer Paul Juon born?

40. Find a portrait and autograph facsimile of Johannes Kepler.

41. The EA, EB 11th and 15th eds. , Chambers and Colliers each emphasize different aspects of the "library." To which would you go for instruction on how to use the library? the service principles and philosophy of librarianship? an historical survey of libraries in America, Britain, and Europe? short accounts of the world's great libraries, library architecture and bibliography?

42. Locate a color photo of limonite, an iron ore.

43. Locate a sketch map of London in Chaucer's time (ca. 1400) based on original records.

44. Cite a brief historical sketch (15-20 lines) of Magdalene College, Cambridge University. What famous English politician bequeathed his library to the college?

45. What is the Chinese game from which the popular 1920's game Mah Jong was adapted?

46. Where was Manon Lescaut first staged and when?

47. What are some of the paintings and illustrations for which Frans Masereel is known?

48.   Where may one find an article on Michigan's "Boy Gov-
      ernor," Steven T. Mason?

49.   Can you find who was governor of Massachusetts in
      1926?

50.   What was the distinctive contribution of Frederick Louis
      Maytag to the state government of Iowa?

51.   What was the duration of the Ming dynasty in China?

52.   Find a picture of Ann Jarvis, who suggested Mother's
      Day.

53.   In which foreign encyclopedia can one find the best maps
      of Napoleon's campaigns?

54.   Locate an illustration of Navajo sand painting.

55.   What was the original name for the city of Washington
      Court House, Ohio?  Why was the present name adopted?

56.   Find a reproduction of the arms of the city of Pau.

57.   Locate a short bibliography (partially annotated) of works
      since 1940 on perfumes and cosmetics.

58.   Where is Iloilo?

59.   What is the elevation of Rib Mountain?   Is it a state
      park?

60.   What was the Ribbon Society?

61.   Find a signed article on the French painter Maurice
      Utrillo.

62.   What was the "grass roots movement" and how was it
      connected with the writings of Fyodor Dostoevsky?

63.   Locate a facsimile of the signature of Jean-Jacques
      Rousseau.

64.   Find a plan of the church of Sancta Sophia in Constan-
      tinople.

65.   Find a portrait of Scanderbeg.

66. Find an article on Albert Schweitzer in any of the encyclopedias.

67. Locate the plans of Seville cathedral and the coat of arms of Sheffield.

68. Where is there a biographical sketch of G. B. Shaw which includes his photograph, his autograph, and a fairly complete list of works by and about him?

69. Cite a monograph on the history of shorthand or stenography showing the alphabets of early British schemes (16th to 18th centuries) and of the Pitman and Gregg systems.

70. Find a ground plan of Solomon's Temple, Jerusalem.

71. What is the color of the body of Sora rail?

72. Who were the Suffetes in Carthaginian politics?

73. What was the reply Thackeray made to a political opponent in an election who had said to Thackeray: "May the best man win"?

74. What is the vernacular name of Tipperary?

75. Ce Tacpatl Mixcoatl's son was a most important figure in Toltec history. What was his name?

76. How many times had the Atlantic been crossed by air before Lindbergh made his solo flight?

77. Find an illustration of Ulysses shooting an arrow into the heart of one of his wife's suitors.

78. Where is there an account of the U.S. Dept. of the Interior which includes both an organization chart and a list of all the secretaries of the department?

79. Identify Agnes Julie Fredrika von Krusenstjerna-Sprengel.

80. Find a summary of the novel The Wandering Jew. Who wrote it?

81. Quote several of George Washington's Rules of Civility.

82.    Find simple diagrammatic illustrations of a water meter
       showing how it works and how to read it.

83.    The Irish and American spelling of whiskey is different
       from the British and Canadian.   What is the Gaelic
       form of the word and what is its meaning?

84.    Who was the commander of the 400 American settlers
       who were massacred in the Wyoming Valley Battle of
       1778?

85.    Find a picture of the "Big Three," Stalin, Churchill,
       and Roosevelt, meeting at Yalta in 1945.

86.    Where could one find both a short definition and a long,
       detailed article on aeronautical engineering?

87.    Where can I find full-color overlays showing the anatomy
       of a grass frog?

88.    Where would you find rules for the card game, skat?

89.    Where would you look to find a picture of the spires of
       the cathedral in Chartres, France?

90.    Where would you find step-by-step instructions for build-
       ing a dam?

91.    Where would you look to find the type of cartoons drawn
       by the Frenchman, Daumier?

92.    Where could you find a colored picture of the state flag,
       flower and bird of Delaware?

93.    Find an article on Albert Einstein with a portrait and
       a signature facsimile.

94.    Where could you find a picture of the Puli working dog?

95.    In what year was the British Ministry of Food amalga-
       mated with the Ministry of Agriculture and Fisheries?

96.    Where could you find the rules for the sport of rugby?

97.    Where would you find pictures of the buildings of interest
       in Frascati, Italy?

98.  Where could you find the real name and a short biography of Cardinale Gaetano?

99.  Locate a picture of a dartboard.

100. Find an illustrated article on the life and culture of ancient Greece with a fact index for young readers.

101. Hathor was a goddess in which mythology?

102. Where could you find a section on history covering both America and the rest of the world with examination questions at the end?

103. What is the name of the curved basket used in the sport of jai alai?

104. Who was Josephus Nelson Larned?

105. Where can I find an article on the April Theses of V. I. Lenin?

106. Middletown, New York was incorporated in what year?

107. Locate a brief discussion of the merits of the paperback novel.

108. Find an article on Wolfgang Mozart with a portrait.

109. What is the pronunciation of Persepolis?

110. Find an identification of "Back Bay" in Boston.

111. For which poem is the English poet, William Shenstone, best known?

112. Where may I find a fairly lengthy entry on Rabelais with a bibliography of works about him?

113. Find a simply written, signed article entitled "How to Do Research," with a list of selected reference books.

114. Find a signed article on trademarks with familiar illustrations and information on United States federal and state trademark laws.

115. Locate an illustrated article for children on the United Nations.

116. Where could you find an outline for the study of the history of the United States?

117. Locate an article on the Vatican with a map and excellent plates.

118. Locate an article about George Washington with numerous illustrations, a copy of his farewell address, and a bibliography of books and films about him.

119. What was named for Bertha Krupp?

120. Find an illustrated article on nursery rhymes with a fact index for young readers.

121. I would like a description, with a map, of the city of Mainz.

122. I want a brief and general explanation of the Haber process.

123. Find the birth date of Julius Caesar.

124. What are the main patterns and colors used in Bulgarian embroidery?

125. What was the title of Virginia Woolf's first novel?

126. What were the inclusive dates of the rule of the House of Stuart over England?

127. Where would you look for a self-educating course on botany?

128. Who was the presidential candidate of the Democratic Party in 1916?

129. What are the three main types of English architecture?

130. How many books are in the New York Public Library?

131. How was the population of the world distributed in the 1500s?

132. What are the names of the important libraries in Florence, Italy?

133.  An instructor is seeking a discussion and perhaps a summary of Diderot's Le Neveu de Rameau, a satire in dialogue.  Can you help him?

134.  A geography student needs to know the location of an island called Crabes in the nineteenth century.

135.  Which book of the Old Testament relates the tale of "The Grateful Dead"?

136.  Where can I find quotations from Voltaire, Rabelais, and Racine?

137.  A political science student needs information about the Finnish Workers' party.  Can you help him?

138.  What caused Pecos Bill's death?

139.  How is the city of Seville arranged?

140.  What are the names and characteristics of several of the newer forms of painting?

141.  What type of dress was worn in the French court around 1430?

142.  Where can I find some historical background on Dieppe prior to the Allied Commando Raid in World War II?

143.  A graduate student is doing research on the official colonial policy immediately prior to the fall of Dien-bienphu.  Where could he look for information?

144.  What painters have done paintings of Stephen the martyr?

145.  What is Napoleon holding in Canova's statue?

146.  A student asks you for a study aid which is in outline form because his friend found one in an encyclopedia, but neither remembers the name of the encyclopedia. Can you help him?

147.  What was the principal event of the year 79 A. D. ?

148.  With which Roman god is the Greek god Zeus identified?

149.  Can you find a table of vertebrates?

150.  A high school student needs a fuller discussion of as-
      teroids than a dictionary contains.  What source would
      provide a simple, nontechnical discussion?

151.  What is the basis of the Islamic calendar?

152.  Find illustrated articles for children on the Indian Wars
      with a list of related articles and a study outline.

153.  Who was called "Old Rough and Ready"?

154.  Who wrote The Damnation of Theron Ware?

155.  What is the length of the Nile River?

156.  Locate articles on Fourier analysis.

157.  Find an article on American life insurance written by
      an expert.

158.  Find a list of how-to-do-it books for the amateur pho-
      tographer.

159.  Find an article on Albia, Iowa.

160.  Locate a long and detailed article on art in the West-
      ern world.

161.  Where are the Beaver Islands?

162.  How is the surname, Campinchi, pronounced?

163.  Find a brief biography of Alfredo Casella, an Italian
      composer who died in 1947.

164.  Find an extensive selection of examination questions
      on the subject of literature.

165.  Find a bibliography on agriculture to be used for self-
      study.

166.  Find a diagram of a tachometer.

167.  Locate a map of Alaska, suitable for children.

168. How is the name of the Aisne River pronounced?

169. How is the word, "calico," pronounced?

170. Find a picture of an adobe hut.

171. Find articles with poems and stories interspersed to capture children's attention.

172. Find an article attempting to help children feel how Eskimos live.

173. Find an illustrated article with several maps and a graded bibliography on North Dakota, suitable for children.

174. Who was Ceres?

175. Find a fact summary in the index of an encyclopedia for the United States with several illustrations suitable for children.

176. Find a brief explanation of Confucianism complete with pronunciation.

177. Locate an in-depth article on Soviet drama.

178. Find an article about the moon designed to capture and hold a child's attention.

179. Find a table of mythological associations.

180. Locate an article on farming aimed at a seventh grade student.

181. Find selected, annotated bibliographies on history, law, political science and government conveniently located in a single volume.

182. Which encyclopedia index provides definitions and basic facts?

183. Who was Gluskabe?

184. Find a study aid in outline form for children.

185. Which encyclopedia has all the articles on biology together?

186.  Find an article for a fifth grade student interested in Italy.

187.  Find an article written from the Communist viewpoint on the Vietnam War.

188.  Which encyclopedia has games, puzzles and riddles for young children?

189.  Find an outline of all knowledge.

190.  Find a colored reproduction of the initial page of "Purgatoria" from Dante's Divine Comedy.

191.  Find a classified bibliography on biology which would be at the junior college level and which would show many facets of the subject, such as "botany," "microbiology," etc. at the end of the set.

192.  Find the date of birth of George Washington in the index of an encyclopedia.

193.  Find a long discussion on sculpture of all times and places with many plates and an extensive bibliography.

194.  Locate a short biography of Melingue, a nineteenth-century French actor and sculptor.

195.  Find a biography of Emerson Hough.

196.  Find an article on the FCC.

197.  Locate an article on the life of Marconi.

198.  Who invented the first successful fountain pen?

199.  Find a list of weights per bushel for various grains and fruits.

200.  Is all of Lower California part of Mexico?

201.  Who was Antoine Lavoisier?

202.  Find an article on the International Red Cross.

203.  Find pictures of various subhuman primates.

204. Find biographies of Roger Bacon and Francis Bacon.

205. How much does one gallon of water weigh?

206. Find a summary of events which occurred in the six-teenth century.

207. Find some general information on Lockport, New York.

208. Find the name of an important person in New York City for a student who needs to make a report on such a person.

209. Who were Laplace and Mayer?

210. What were the names of Henry VIII's wives?

211. Who was Queen Victoria's mother?

212. Find a biography of Patrick Henry for a child.

213. Find an article on fate and free will.

214. Find a description of life on Southern plantations for a child.

215. Find a biography of Max Planck.

216. What is the largest bell in the world?

217. What is the meaning of "Israfel"?

218. Find an article on the Imperial Valley.

219. Find an article on H. Sienkiewicz.

220. Find a picture of Martin Luther.

221. Where is St. Paul's Cathedral?

222. Find a short method of figuring interest.

223. Is Michigan an Indian word and what is the meaning?

224. Who was the Man in the Iron Mask?

225. Who were Héloise and Abélard?

226.  Identify Eli Metchnikoff.

227.  Identify Nizam al Mulk.

228.  What is the longest river in the world?

229.  Were the Swedes Mongols?

230.  How does one figure extra cube roots by logarithms?

231.  How long does it take a baby elephant to mature?

232.  Which is harder, glass or steel?

233.  Who was Alexander VI?

234.  What is the national flower of Scotland?

235.  What are the true colors of the peacock?

236.  Find a picture of a Dutch windmill.

237.  Compare rainfall in England and France.

238.  Find some information on cavemen appropriate for children.

239.  What part of the United States produces the most cranberries?

240.  Find an article on cocoa.

241.  Find a history of the X-ray.

242.  In what year was Albert Einstein born?

243.  How is steel processed?

244.  Find a short history of Sweden.

245.  Locate a history of national parks.

246.  Find a picture of a fawn.

247.  Find a biography of Willa Cather.

248.  Do penguins have feathers on their flippers?

249.    Find instructions on how to form Roman numerals through 500.

250.    Find a biography of James Bright.

251.    Who was the first United States president not born a British subject?

252.    What were the names of Admiral Peary's ships?

253.    Find a general article on silkworms.

254.    Find a history of ballet in Australia.

255.    For what is Trinidad noted?

256.    Locate pictures of flags from Latin American countries.

257.    What is the abbreviation for London?

258.    What is the name of the red cape used in bull fighting?

259.    What are the major sports in England?

260.    What was the date when Hitler invaded Poland?

261.    What are the most important provisions of the Magna Carta, the Bill of Rights, and the Petition of Rights?

262.    Find some information on the role of Canada in World War I.

263.    What is the word for a polygon of nine sides?

264.    Find a picture of the chambered nautilus showing the chambers.

265.    Find a biography of Woodrow Wilson for a small boy.

266.    Find a biography of John Rutledge.

267.    What did Florence Nightingale wear during the Crimean War?

268.    Find pictures of gypsies' costumes.

269.    What was the birthplace of the former Senator Townsend?

270.  Who painted "Napoleon Visiting the Pest House at Jaffa"?

271.  Why do people throw rice at weddings?

272.  Find a list of the state birds and flowers.

273.  Find information on the Leni-Lenape tribe of Indians.

274.  Locate information on the port of Huelva in Spain.

275.  Find a map showing the resources of New Jersey.

276.  When did Henry Ford die?

277.  When did Franklin Roosevelt die?

278.  Find a history of the game of bridge.

279.  Where was Ernie Pyle killed?

280.  What are the requirements for membership in the American Legion?

281.  What were the major causes of World War I?

282.  What are the procedures for a trial by jury?

283.  When was the first rural mail delivery?

284.  Find data on videodisks.

285.  Which encyclopedia has a "Colorpedia"?

286.  Locate an article on "iconoclasm" appropriate for a junior high school student.


Reference Materials

Academic American Encyclopedia
Britannica Junior Encyclopaedia
Brockhaus Enzyklopaedie
Chambers's Encyclopaedia
Childcraft

Collier's Encyclopedia
Compton's Encyclopedia
Compton's Precyclopedia
Enciclopedia italiana di scienze, lettere ed arti
Enciclopedia universal ilustrada Europeo-Americana (Espasa)
Encyclopaedia Britannica
Encyclopedia Americana
La grande encyclopédie
Grand-Larousse encyclopédique
Great Soviet Encyclopedia
Lincoln Library of Essential Information
Merit Students Encyclopedia
New Century Cyclopedia of Names
New Columbia Encyclopedia
Random House Encyclopedia
World Book Encyclopedia

CHAPTER 2


YEARBOOKS


Reference Interviews


Patron #1.  A man.

Patron:          I need your help with three questions.   First,
                 I'd like to know the number of square miles in
                 the U. S. and Canada.
Librarian:       Do you want the U. S. with Hawaii and Alaska or
                 just the 48 states?
Patron:          Could I have both?
Librarian:       It's also divided by land and water.   Do you
                 want it together or divided?
Patron:          Divided.   Now, do you have the area of the
                 Great Lakes?
Librarian:       Do you want the area of the drainage basin or
                 just the water?
Patron:          Just the water.
Librarian:       Are you using these figures for a paper or some-
                 thing?
Patron:          Yes, I'm comparing the population of certain
                 states as a percentage of the total land area and
                 population.   Now I need the population of the
                 U. S. and Canada--the most recent figures pos-
                 sible.

                 Which sources would you check to answer these
                 questions?


Patron #2.  A college student.

| | |
|---|---|
| Patron: | I want to find some information on McCormick Place. |
| Librarian: | Is that a building? |
| Patron: | Yes. |
| Librarian: | Do you know where it's located? |
| Patron: | Chicago. |
| Librarian: | Just what did you want to know about the building? |
| Patron: | I'd like to know when it burned down. |
| Librarian: | Do you have any general idea of how recently this happened? |
| Patron: | In this century. |

Where would you look?

**Patron #3.    A man.**

| | |
|---|---|
| Patron: | Did Michigan go to Pasadena in 1967? |
| Librarian: | You mean did The University of Michigan go to the Rose Bowl in 1967? |
| Patron: | Yes. |

Where would you look?

**Patron #4.    A junior high school boy.**

| | |
|---|---|
| Patron: | Do you have any lists of prizes? |
| Librarian: | What sort of prizes do you mean?  Suggestions for party prizes or what? |
| Patron: | Well, you see, I've got this list of guys--scientists and authors--and they won prizes, Nobel and Pulitzer, and I've got to find out when they won them. |

Where could the dates be found?

**Patron #5.    A student.**

| | |
|---|---|
| Patron: | I would like to know where I can find the results of the 1968 national election for President of the United States. |
| Librarian: | Is this for your government class? |
| Patron: | Yes, and I would like to know about the unsuccessful candidates, too, and the names of the other parties. |

Librarian:   Oh, you mean like the Socialist Party?
Patron:      Yes.

             Where could this information be found?


Patron #6.  A high school student.

Patron:      Where can I find a short article on Somaliland?
Librarian:   You don't want to use the encyclopedias?
Patron:      No, those articles are too long.

             Where would you look for brief information?


Patron #7.  A man.

Patron:      Where could I find the population of some cities?
Librarian:   Which cities?
Patron:      Some of the large cities in the U.S., like De-
             troit and Cleveland.

             Where would you look?


## Reference Questions


1.  Find the address of the American Medical Association.

2.  What is the Jewish population of Argentina?

3.  Name the U.N. representatives from Japan.

4.  Who is the chair of the British Broadcasting Corpor-
    ation?

5.  Did Babe Ruth ever hit 60 home runs in one year?

6.  Who is the leader of the Communist party in Australia?

7.  Where is there the most complete list of newspapers and
    magazines published in British Columbia?

8.  Who is the keeper of Oriental Printed Books and Manu-
    scripts in the British Library?

9.  Find a list of Cuba's national holidays.

10. What are the names and addresses of the newspapers and periodicals published in Ceylon?

11. Which country produces the most wool?

12. What are the annual fees at Eton College in Windsor, England?

13. Locate a brief summary of the history of dictatorships in Central America.

14. What are the major sources of revenue of Gibraltar?

15. What is the vernacular name of the Hashemite kingdom of Jordan?

16. What is the highest building in the world?

17. What are some of the major banks of Iceland?

18. What are the gasoline taxes in Illinois?

19. What is the maximun number of representatives in India's House of People?

20. In terms of membership, which are the biggest churches in Ireland, and what are the names of their chief officers?

21. How many telephones are there in Japan?

22. When did the English pirate Sharpe sack La Serena, Chile?

23. Which public libraries are members of the Yukon Regional Library System?

24. What is the address of the Librairie Ernest Flammarion in Paris?

25. Find a brief history and description of the Victoria Cross medal of honor.

26. What is the lowest temperature on record in Minneapolis?

27. What is the height of Mt. Everest?

28.  Who is the director of the National Gallery in London?

29.  What are the inheritance taxes in the State of New Jersey?

30.  What is the address of Martinus Nijhoff's publishing firm at The Hague?

31.  How many Presidents of the U. S. have received Nobel Prizes?

32.  How many motor vehicles are registered in Nova Scotia?

33.  Who were the Poets Laureate of England in the 17th century?

34.  What is the full title of the Pope?

35.  What are the chief Portuguese insurance companies?

36.  Locate a perpetual calendar which covers the dates January 1st, 1 A.D. to December 31st, 2000 A.D. On which day of the week will April 17, 1990 fall?

37.  When does the month of Ramadan begin this year?

38.  What is the Roman numeral for 1,000,000?

39.  What is the Indian rupee worth in American money? What other coins are used in India?

40.  What is the population of the capital of Saudi Arabia?

41.  What is Sikkim and how large is it?

42.  What is the national anthem of Spain?

43.  In what cities are the Sugar Bowl and the Orange Bowl played?

44.  Who holds the title of Duke of St. Alban's?

45.  Find the text of the Charter of the United Nations.

46.  What is the address of the Universal Postal Union?

47.  Find a list of the administrative officials and faculty of the University of New Brunswick.

48. Who was the first occupant of the White House?

49. How is a woman's rank determined in the order of precedence in England?

50. What is the name of the present Archbishop of Canterbury?

51. What is the address of the Canadian embassy in Burma?

52. Locate a series of star maps which charts the movement of the constellations for January to December.

53. What important events took place in horse racing in Britain two years ago?

54. Where could you find the name of the president and present address of the Eaton Insurance Company of Toronto, Canada?

55. What are the names of the political parties in Luxembourg?

56. Find a chart showing Postmaster Generals by administration, George Washington to the present?

57. Where could one find recent statistics on transportation in Canada?

58. What important matters were discussed at the United Nations last year?

59. Does the U. S. S. R. have an embassy in Upper Volta?

60. What is the traditional dinner hour of Uruguay?

61. What are the annuities paid various members of the Royal Family of England?

62. I would like a daily chronology of the major world events for a given year in the past decade.

63. How many people in Ontario are employed in the fishing industry?

64. Who are the delegates to the Economic and Social Council of the United Nations?

65.  What are the names of the representatives of Tunisia to Great Britain?

66.  What is the orbital velocity and the synodical period of Mercury?

67.  What is the type of government of Morocco?

68.  How many telephones (per 100 population) are there in Canada?

69.  Who is the president of Zambia?

70.  Who won the Nobel Prize in physics last year?

71.  Where can I find a description of Caracas?

72.  Who is the President of the Canadian Pacific Railway?

73.  Do you have a copy of the text of the Tashkent Declaration signed by Shastri before he died?

74.  What is the population of the city of Birmingham, England, and who is its Lord Mayor?

75.  Where is there a list of the countries in which Spain maintains diplomatic representatives?

76.  Who is the honorary president of the Presidium of the World Council of Churches?

77.  At what time will the sun rise in Ottawa on November 6?

78.  What major changes took place last year in the Swiss economy?

79.  Who was awarded the Nobel Prizes in Chemistry last year?

80.  Find the address of the International Bar Association.

81.  What is the name of the leading newspaper in Oslo, Norway?

82.  Where can I find statistics on the production of fur in Canada?

83.   What is the high and low tide for the coastal city of
      Aberdeen, Scotland?

84.   Who is the Ambassador of Belgium to Canada?

85.   What is the Gross National Product of Gabon?

86.   Who is the Postmaster-General of Great Britain and
      what is his salary?

87.   I am going to be making a trip to Lima, Peru in Oc-
      tober.  I plan to be there for two months.  What sort
      of clothes should I take?

88.   Can you tell me where I might find a description of the
      various government agencies which are conducting sur-
      veying and mapping in Canada?

89.   Where can one find information on the World Council
      of Churches?

90.   Where can one find information on the North Atlantic
      Treaty Organization?

91.   What are the principal industries of Iraq?

92.   What is the amount of pay of a vice-admiral in the Navy
      with twelve years of service?

93.   Which major city of the United States contains the most
      sodium in its drinking water?

94.   Find an article on last year's domestic events in Iran
      with a brief summary of data on that country.

95.   Locate a world survey of last year's literature presented
      by country.

96.   What percentage of Danes were born in Denmark?

97.   Locate an overview of the judicial system in the Nether-
      lands.

98.   Find the name of a Jamaican opera company.

99.   How do Australia's Liberal Party and Country Party
      differ?

100. Is The Times of India a Nationalist newspaper?

101. Where would you find a short history of Tobago?

102. Find a list of museums in Kingston, Jamaica.

103. Is the tap water safe to drink in the Netherlands Antilles?

104. Does Portugal use the metric system?

105. What are the world's top fifty banks?

106. Where may I find brief information about banking in Canada?

107. What was the major literary event of the Western world between 900-800 B.C. ?

108. What are the areas of specialty of the Peabody Museum?

109. Who are Algeria's cabinet members?

110. Locate information on education in Nauru.

111. What were the results of the last general election in Belgium?

112. Locate a street map of Rio de Janeiro.

113. Locate a news summary of the last New York Democratic primary.

114. Locate the scores of the World Series games from 1903 to the present.

115. What is the currency of Norway?

116. What are the programs of Malta's two leading political parties?

117. Who won the first Indianapolis 500 race?

118. What is the predominant religion in Afghanistan?

119. When is the rainy season in Trinidad?

120. Which country produced the most steel last year?

121.  How many ships are in Sri Lanka's navy?

122.  Who are the assistant bishops at Canterbury?

123.  Find a map of La Paz, Bolivia, with a discussion of points of interest.

124.  Which players have won the Grand Slam of Tennis? What requirements must be met to earn this honor?

125.  Find a list of educational institutions and their staffs in Canada.

126.  What is the total value of food imported into Finland?

127.  What was the date when the bridge between Padukah, Kentucky and Bridgeport, Illinois was opened?

128.  Who is the United States ambassador to the Soviet Union?

129.  What are some of the new plays which have opened in New York recently?

130.  Who are the Senators and Representatives from New York?

131.  How many Confucianists live in Fiji?

132.  Find a picture of the flag of the President of the United States.

133.  Find a list of weights and measures in Great Britain.

134.  What is the evening star now?

135.  How long was Alfred the Great king of England?

136.  Locate some information about fraternities.

137.  Who is the chairperson of the American Red Cross?

138.  When did the United States adopt woman's suffrage?

139.  What is the religion of Pakistan?

140.  What is the capital of Oregon?

141.  Find a list of state governors.

142.  What is the postage to foreign countries?

143.  Find a list of the cabinet officers.

144.  Where is the largest telescope in the world?

145.  What are the rules for the proper display of the American flag?

146.  Who was the third Vice-President of the United States and what was his political affiliation?

147.  Can the son of a President be elected President?

148.  How has the cost of living risen for the past ten years?

149.  What is the average yearly salary for teachers in the United States.

150.  What is the deepest oil well in the world?

151.  What gifts are appropriate for a thirtieth wedding anniversary?

152.  On what day in 1791 did The Bill of Rights go into effect?

153.  When will Easter be next year?

154.  When was Easter in 1924?

155.  What are the largest public libraries in the United States?

156.  What was the date of the first Tuesday after the first Monday in 1942?

157.  What is the state emblem of California?

158.  Who is the Speaker of the House of Representatives?

159.  What are the names of the New Jersey Representatives in the United States Congress?

160.  Is John "Blood" McNally in the Pro Football Hall of Fame?

161.   Find a summary of the 1790 census of New York state.

162.   What is the population of Cleveland?

163.   What is the date, MDCCCXCIV?

164.   What are the names of the associate justices of the
       United States Supreme Court?

165.   When has the United States declared war against var-
       ious countries?

166.   Find a list of national holidays of the United States?

167.   What is the public debt of the United States?

168.   Find summaries of divorce laws in various states.

169.   Which of the Great Lakes is the largest?

170.   Which athlete earned the most money last year?

171.   Locate the flag of the United Nations.

172.   Find a picture of the flag of India.

173.   Locate the exact wording of the Pledge of Allegiance.

174.   When was the National Speleological Society formed?

175.   What are the ten largest cities in the United States?

176.   What is the postal rate on books?

177.   What was the maiden name of Millard Fillmore's first
       wife?

178.   What is the meaning of a dash over a Roman numeral?

179.   When is Flag Day?

180.   What are the marriage laws in Indiana?

181.   What were the principal events 100 years ago?

182.   What is the fifteenth wedding anniversary called?

183.   What is the origin of the names of the states?

184. How do the various states compare in National Forests?

185. What is the value of a peso?

186. What are the names of the National Memorials?

187. What are the gasoline taxes in the various states?

188. How many time zones does Greenland have?

189. What is the largest dam in the world?

190. How old is the monarch of the Netherlands?

191. Find a list of all the Senators and Representatives in the present Congress.

192. Does Portugal produce more wine than olive oil?

193. What are the names of the hotels in Morelia, Mexico?

194. What years was Chester Arthur president?

195. What are the immigration laws of the United States?

196. Who have won the Pulitzer prizes for the past ten years?

197. Find the text of the Declaration of Independence.

198. What is the ratio of divorces to marriages?

199. How many electoral votes does Illinois have?

200. How many people are enrolled in Blue Cross?

201. How often does Tuttle's Comet reappear to Earth observers?

202. How much money was appropriated for defense by the last Congress?

203. How many stripes does the Coast Guard insignia for an ensign carry?

204. What is the boiling point of alcohol?

205. Can Easter ever be on March 29?

206. What New York plays have had the longest runs?

207. What magazine has the largest circulation?

208. Locate a list of geologic periods.

209. What is the record high and low in temperature for Miami?

210. What are the territories and dependencies of the United States?

211. What are the average teachers' salaries, broken down by states?

212. Where in New York is the Hall of Fame?

213. What is the name of the Congressman from this district?

214. How long is the Alaskan Highway?

215. How many accidental deaths were there last year in the United States?

216. Find a list of famous planetariums.

217. What is the name of the national anthem of Sweden?

218. How many Indians are there in the United States, by state?

219. Find a list of famous fires.

220. What was the increase of the black population in the United States from the first census to the Civil War?

221. What was the date of the Cocoanut Grove fire?

222. Was Hannibal Hamlin ever Vice-President of the U.S.?

223. Find information on an event which happened in the United States a month ago.

224. Who is the current director of public records for Great Britain?

225.    What is the platform of the Australian Labor Party?

226.    What are the names of the foreign banks which have
        branch offices in Japan?

227.    On what date will Easter be observed next year?

228.    What were some of the major events in the coal in-
        dustry last year?

229.    What were some of the major events in Britain last
        month?

## Reference Materials

Americana Annual
Annual Register of World Events
Britannica Book of the Year
Canada Year Book
Canadian Almanac and Directory
Collier's Yearbook
Compton Yearbook
Europa Year Book
Facts on File
Information Please Almanac
International Yearbook and Statesmen's Who's Who
Keesing's Contemporary Archives
Political Handbook and Atlas of the World
South American Handbook
Statesman's Year-Book
Whitaker's Almanac
World Almanac
World Book Year Book
Yearbook of the United Nations

CHAPTER 3

## STATISTICAL SOURCES

### Reference Interviews

Patron #1.  A woman.

Patron:       I need information on budgets.
Librarian:   How to make a budget or statistics on budgets?
Patron:       What I want is something on budgets for fami-
              lies; statistics, I guess.
Librarian:   Then you want budget figures for families in the
              United States?
Patron:       Well, I don't really know.   You see, I'm having
              an argument, discussion really, with my husband
              on how much money we should spend on different
              things, and I thought if I could find out what other
              families like us spend to live comfortably it would
              help me to win.

              Where would you look for this information?


Patron #2.  A young high school girl.

Patron:       I need to find some election results.
Librarian:   Do you need to have state or federal election
              results?
Patron:       I need them for the election of Madison.
Librarian:   Let's see.   That was 18--?
Patron:       It was in 1812.
Librarian:   You want the election results for the presidential
              election of 1812.   Do you just want the total
              electoral vote or state by state?

Patron:        I need the state by state vote.

               Where could this information be found?


Patron #3.     A student.

Patron:        Where can I find statistics on immigration?
Librarian:     Do you want statistical quotas from countries
               or do you want actual immigrants admitted from
               all countries or both?
Patron:        I want information on actual immigrants admitted
               from all countries.

               Where would you look?



## Reference Questions

1.  What was the estimated population of the American col-
    onies in 1630?

2.  What was the average population per household in Ann
    Arbor in 1970?

3.  What was the death rate among the male population of
    Massachusetts in 1895?

4.  What was the number of German immigrants from 1850-
    1870?

5.  How many Lithuanian immigrants were living in the United
    States in 1850?

6.  How many marriages took place in Alaska and New York
    in 1960 and 1970?

7.  How much money was spent by the Navy Department in
    1792?

8.  Does Portland, Maine have more clear days during the
    year than Detroit?

9.  What was the tonnage of sailing vessels of the U.S. Mer-
    chant Marine in 1866?

10.  How much did the federal government spend on national
     defense in 1942?

11.  What was the development cost for civilian atomic energy
     power reactors last year?

12.  What is the average number of people in a household
     in Paraguay?

13.  Find general statistics about the characteristics of new,
     privately-owned one family homes in the United States
     which are fairly recent.

14.  What is the average August temperature of Philadelphia?

15.  What was the population of the Standard Metropolitan
     Areas in the last census of the U. S. ?

16.  Find the figures for unemployment in the first half of
     the twentieth century in the U. S.

17.  Find the average income for an industrial worker in
     1930 in the U. S.

18.  What is the voting population of California?

19.  What is the divorce rate in Japan?

20.  Find the number of Chinese immigrants to the U. S. in
     1850.

21.  How many institutions of higher education were there
     in the U. S. in 1946?

22.  What was the population of New York City in 1900?

23.  How many acres of sugar beets are harvested annually
     in the U. S. ?

24.  Where could I find a list of money conversion co-efficients
     and factors?

25.  What was the amount of the total defense contract awards
     made last year in the U. S. ?

26.  What is the amount of coffee production in Uganda?

27.  What was the number of pounds of raw silk exported from North and South Carolina in 1750?

28.  What was the total income of U. S. life insurance companies in 1898?

29.  What is the population of Prokopyesk, Russia?

30.  What was the average farm wage, per month, in the U. S. in 1920 for a hand living with a farmer?

31.  Which is more populous: Argentina, Colombia, or Burma?

32.  What was the population of the U. S. in 1962?

33.  How many telephones are in use in Belgium?

34.  What was the average annual salary of college teachers in the U. S. in 1940?

35.  What is the birth rate in Sweden?

36.  What was the average number of rooms of a new, one-family home in the U. S. in 1950?

37.  How many tons of tin were produced in Bolivia two years ago?

38.  What is the average life expentancy for men in India?

39.  How many doctoral degrees in psychology were conferred by U. S. institutions in 1981? What percent of the recipients were female?

40.  How many renter-occupied housing units with more than one bathroom are there in Albany, New York?

41.  How many non-whites own their own farms in Rhode Island?

42.  What were the average annual earnings per full-time employee in the United States by major industry for 1938?

43.  What was the acreage of oats harvested for 1926-30 in the United States?

44. How many banks were there in the United States in 1933?

45. How many gasoline service stations are there in Rapid City, South Dakota?

46. What was the retail value of microwave ovens produced in the U. S. in 1978?

47. How many Methodists were there in the United States in 1936?

48. Find the population of Santa Monica, California for each decade since 1890.

49. What is the average age at marriage for a male in New Zealand?

50. How much beer was produced in New Zealand each year for the past ten years?

51. What was China's crude death rate in 1935?

52. What was the price of lead in the United Kingdom month before last?

53. How many Indians are there in Michigan?

54. What are the age and population characteristics of this county?

55. How many black people live in Pike County, Ohio?

56. How many people who are over eighteen live in this county?

57. How many Turks live in European Turkey?

58. Find the most recent figures available on unemployment in Denmark, Finland, and Sweden.

59. How many Germans immigrated to this country between 1850 and 1870?

60. What is the total median income of families living in the South Atlantic states?

61. What is the average number of rooms per housing unit in the city of Laredo, Texas?

62.   What is the college enrollment in New Jersey by county?

63.   How many acres of forest land were burned in the United
      States in forest fires in 1933?

64.   What were some of the major publications of the U. S.
      government on statistics on employment last year?

65.   How can I find statistics published in Forbes magazine
      last year?

66.   What is the average number of years of education com-
      pleted by people in this congressional district?


## Reference Materials


American Statistics Index
Census of the U. S.
Congressional District Data Book
County and City Data Book
Demographic Yearbook
Economic Almanac
Historical Statistics of the United States
Statistical Abstract of the United States
Statistical Reference Index
United Nations.   Monthly Bulletin of Statistics
United Nations.   Statistical Yearbook

# CHAPTER 4

## BIOGRAPHICAL SOURCES

### Reference Interviews

<u>Patron #1.</u>   A high school boy.

| | |
|---|---|
| Patron: | Where is your section on Stephen Crane? |
| Librarian: | Do you know what nationality he is? |
| Patron: | I don't know.  He was a writer. |
| Librarian: | We can find out from Benet's <u>Reader's Encyclopedia</u>.  It says he was an American, and lived from 1871-1900. |
| Patron: | That's what I thought.  We're studying American literature. |
| Librarian: | Did you want books to check out on him, or reference books to look at here? |
| Patron: | Stuff to look at here, I guess.  The report's due tomorrow. |

What would you suggest?

<u>Patron #2.</u>   A woman.

| | |
|---|---|
| Patron: | Where could I find some biographical information on S. S. Kresge?  I already checked <u>Current Biography</u>.  He isn't listed. |
| Librarian: | You could check for references to articles. |

Where would you look?

<u>Patron #3.</u>   A high school boy.

Patron:        Where should I go to find out about authors?
Librarian:     Do you mean as a profession or did you have
               one specific author in mind?
Patron:        Just one--Forest McDonald.
Librarian:     Is he still alive?
Patron:        I don't know.
Librarian:     Well, when did he write a book that you know
               of?
Patron:        The one I'm reading was copyrighted in 1958.
Librarian:     Is he an American then?
Patron:        Yes, I think so.  At least it was published in
               the United States.

               Where would you go for information?


Patron #4.    A woman.

Patron:        Where do I find biographies of Americans?
Librarian:     We have several sources.  Which person did
               you have in mind?
Patron:        Gordy Howe.
Librarian:     The hockey player?
Patron:        Yes.
Librarian:     Did you want a long or short article?
Patron:        Something longer, descriptive.

               Where would you find lengthy articles?


Patron #5.    A college-aged boy.

Patron:        Do you have any books about motion pictures?
Librarian:     Yes, we have.  I'll show them to you.
Patron:        Well, I don't see what I'm looking for in here.
               This is a difficult subject.  I need some infor-
               mation about Akira Kurosawa.
Librarian:     I'm sorry to say that I don't recognize that name.
               Who is he?
Patron:        He's a movie director.
Librarian:     What nationality is he and is he living?
Patron:        Oh yes, he's alive.  He's Japanese.  I'm taking
               a course in the theater and I have to have some
               information about this guy.  Not too much; enough
               for a two-page report.

               Where would you check?

Patron #6.   A young high school girl.

Patron:       My teacher has assigned each of us a contempor-
              ary author to write on.   Mine is Agatha Christie.
              Where should I start looking?
Librarian:    Did you check the card catalog?
Patron:       Yes, they didn't have any works on her--just by
              her.
Librarian:    Contemporary Authors would be the next logical
              place to look.
Patron:       There isn't anything on her.

              Where would you go to next?


Patron #7.   A high school boy.

Patron:       Where do you keep books on American authors?
Librarian:    Did you have a specific author in mind?
Patron:       Yes.   Faulkner.
Librarian:    Did you want a biography or a criticism?
Patron:       Criticism.   I'm writing this paper.
Librarian:    Do you want to criticize a specific work then,
              or Faulkner's work in general?
Patron:       Just a couple of his novels.
Librarian:    Did you check the card catalog under Faulkner?
Patron:       Yes, but I don't know which books are good for
              what I want.   What I really want is a list of es-
              says.

              What would you suggest?


Patron #8.   A high school girl.

Patron:       I need some information on Nelson Rockefeller.
Librarian:    What kind of information do you want?
Patron:       I just want something brief.   I don't want to read
              a book or anything.
Librarian:    Do you want something general on his life or
              something more specific on his political career
              and views?
Patron:       I want something very brief just on his life.

              Where would you look?


Patron #9.   A high school girl.

| Patron: | I need to find out the name of a legislator from 1789 to 1800. |
| Librarian: | Is this the U. S. Congress or some state legislature that you have in mind? |
| Patron: | The U. S. Congress.   Both houses. |
| Librarian: | Do you want the name of just any one who was a legislator or a list of all of them? |
| Patron: | I want to see a list of all of them so that I can pick one to write a term paper on. |

Where would you find a list?


**Patron #10.** A high school boy.

| Patron: | I have to know about Karl Gauss. |
| Librarian: | What class is this for? |
| Patron: | Math. |
| Librarian: | Is he a mathematician? |
| Patron: | My teacher said he was a great mathematician who died sometime in the 1800's. |
| Librarian: | Was he an American? |
| Patron: | No.   He was from Germany. |

Where would you find a brief biography?


**Patron #11.** A woman.

| Patron: | I just saw Loves of Isadora and I want to know when she was born. |
| Librarian: | Her full name was Isadora Duncan. |
| Patron: | That's right. |

Where would you find the date?


**Patron #12.** A student.

| Patron: | I want to know where I can find a critical essay on "The Duty of Civil Disobedience." |
| Librarian: | Who wrote it? |
| Patron: | It doesn't matter.   I just need an essay. |

Where would you look?


**Patron #13.** A high school boy.

| Patron: | This book has only a paragraph on Donald McKay. Where can I get more on him? |
| Librarian: | Is he an American? |
| Patron: | Yes. |
| Librarian: | Dead? |
| Patron: | Yes. |

Where would you look?

**Patron #14.** A high school student.

| Patron: | I have to find out about Isaiah Thomas.  Where can I look? |
| Librarian: | How much information do you need? |
| Patron: | I just need a little information about who he was, where he lived, when he was born.  I don't want to read a whole book. |
| Librarian: | Was he American? |
| Patron: | Yes. |
| Librarian: | Do you know when he lived? |
| Patron: | I'm not sure, but I think in the colonial period. |

Where could you locate this information?

**Patron #15.** A student.

| Patron: | Do you have anything on British authors? |
| Librarian: | Did you want a general work or a specific author? |
| Patron: | What I'm looking for is a biography of Shelley. |

What would you suggest?

**Patron #16.** A student.

| Patron: | I am writing a paper about J. D. Salinger and I don't know where to look for information. |
| Librarian: | Were you interested in any specific work of the author or a general discussion of his life and work? |
| Patron: | Just a general discussion, but I want to bring in his work and some criticism, too. |

Where would you go for biographies and critical articles?

## Reference Questions

1. Find the publishing history of Anne Bradstreet's poetry?

2. Was Marie Emma Lajeunesse Albani's last name her maiden name, or married name?

3. Name several famous students of the educator Benjamin Abbot.

4. Who was the first rabbi to be ordained in the U. S. ?

5. What is the correct pronunciation of the name Alaud-din, second king of the Kilji dynasty of India?

6. Who was Antonio Alaminos?

7. Who was the mayor of Albany, N. Y. in 1796?

8. When was Count Anckwitz born?

9. When did the historian Bernard Andre live and what was his important work?

10. Who was the first president of Antioch College?

11. Locate biographical material on Francis of Assisi that would be suitable for children.

12. What is the family name of Lord Beaverbrook?

13. What is the date of birth of Georges Bidault?

14. Who received the Brewster medal in 1921?

15. Who was governor of California in 1911?

16. Who was the first Roman Catholic bishop of the Archdiocese of Baltimore?

17. What are the chief works of Louis Ferdinand Céline?

18. Where was Frances Bano Chance born?

19. Who was the founder of the first county jail library?

20. Name several noteworthy legal annotators born in the U. S.

21.  Who are some of the most distinguished American con-
     ductors of the past?

22.  Who was Speaker of the House in the 73rd Congress,
     1933?

23.  Who got the Congressional Gold Medal in 1777 for the
     surrender of Burgoyne?

24.  Who was U. S. Ambassador to Costa Rica in 1853?

25.  What was the title of Richard Crashaw's first volume of
     poetry?

26.  Find a biography of Arthur R. Cushny, died 1926, for-
     merly of The University of Michigan.

27.  Who wrote a book about composers containing a discus-
     sion of Ingolf Dahl?  It was titled U. S. Composers or
     North American Composers, the patron believes.

28.  What library magazine carried an obituary of Test Dal-
     ton in 1946?

29.  What was the War of the Dictionaries?

30.  What is the importance of Paul A. Dirac?

31.  Find a facsimile of Walt Disney's signature.

32.  When was Douglas Fairbanks' picture The Black Pirate
     produced?

33.  Who was the maternal grandfather of Samuel Fairclough,
     nonconformist divine?

34.  What are the publications of Max Forster?

35.  What scientific work was done by Ferdinand André Fou-
     qué?

36.  Did Eleanor Everest Freer write an opera about Pan-
     dora?

37.  What was the real name of the American actress "Lotta"?

38.  Where did Thomas W. F. Gann, the British archeologist,
     receive his early training?

39. Dave Garroway published and sold some book or pamphlet before he became famous.   What was its title?

40. Can you locate the article about Kid Gavilan written by J. Lardner?

41. What statue by Johannes S. Gelert can be seen in Battle Creek, Michigan?

42. Who were some of the outstanding geographers in the U. S. in the 19th century?

43. Who received the Willard Gibbs Medal for 1930?

44. Where was James Riddle Goffe born?

45. Were any famous Americans born in Greece?

46. Who designed the Hell Gate Bridge in New York?

47. Locate a brief sampling of Lucretia Davidson's poetry.

48. Find a portrait of Josiah G. Holland, first editor of Scribner's Monthly.

49. Who were the U. S. Senators from Illinois in 1850?

50. Find a portrait of Burl Ives.

51. Did Thomas Jacomb write a book on the 7th chapter of Romans?

52. What was the early life of Albert Sidney Johnston? Where can one find further biographical material about him?

53. Locate an article on Alice Cunningham Fletcher, American ethnologist, which provides numerous citations to other biographical sources.

54. Find a portrait of Jennifer Jones.

55. What was the relationship of Mrs. Charles Kean, the actress, to Charles Tree?

56. What can you find concerning Florence Kelley, who died in the 1930's?

57. Where did William C. Kendall, the naturalist, receive his education?

58. In what colleges did William P. Ker teach?

59. Did Henry Churchill King wear glasses?

60. How old was David Kinnison when he died?

61. What famous Americans went to Knox College?

62. For what was Leonard Knyff principally known?

63. What Americans have received the Laetare Medal?

64. Who was the first American manufacturer of the anvil?

65. Who were some of the important librarians in the U. S. in the 19th century?

66. What were the highlights in the life of Francis J. Lippitt?

67. Can you find a portrait of Arthur Cushman McGiffert?

68. Where did Archibald MacLeish go to college?

69. What has been the career of General A. G. L. McNaughton of Canada?

70. What book designing has been done by Paul McPharlin?

71. Who is called the father of American map making?

72. Who was Juan Ruíz d'Alarcon y Mendoza?

73. Where was Anastas Mikoyan born?

74. In what century did Johann Jakob Mnioch live?

75. What was the occupation of Leopold Seyffert, born in California in 1888?

76. Who was Allen G. Newman?

77. What was the business of John Howard Nodal's father?

78. How did the American singer Nordica happen to take this name?

79. When did Paul Ambrose Oliver die?

80. Who was Jacobus Oud?

81. Who was Secretary of War in Polk's administration?

82. Who was the first Bishop of the Protestant Episcopal Church in the U. S. ?

83. Can you find a biographical sketch of Sir Walter A. Raleigh? Where can a picture of him be found?

84. Find a portrait of Gertrude Rand, the psychologist.

85. What was Jacob Rayman's profession?

86. Had Paul Robeson played Othello before 1944?

87. How is the name Ruthven pronounced in Scotland?

88. What was the career of John Drew Salmon?

89. Who was president pro tem of the Senate of the U. S. in 1815?

90. For what accomplishment is Nellie Ross remembered?

91. When was C. Aubrey Smith knighted?

92. What are the birth and death dates of Godfrey Thring?

93. Locate a list of published works written by Margaret Truman.

94. Were any famous Americans born in Turkey?

95. Who was the first woman member of the clergy in the Unitarian Church?

96. What was the original spelling of William Faulkner's surname?

97. In what year did T. S. Eliot receive the Nobel Prize for literature?

98. Where was Thornton Wilder born?

99. What famous Americans went to William and Mary College?

100. What was the profession of Thomas Burks Yuille, who died in 1934?

101. Locate a lengthy, signed biography of President John Adams, with a bibliography of works about him.

102. What is the address of the Soviet foreign trade official, Aziz Aga-Aga-bab Alekperov?

103. Where could you find a scholarly article with a bibliography about Samuel Barron, the Confederate naval officer?

104. In what sources can biographies of Pietro Cavallini be found?

105. What is the title of Aleksandr Solzhenitsyn's autobiography?

106. Locate a portrait and autograph of David Crockett, the American who died defending the Alamo.

107. What is the correct pronunciation of John Donne's last name?

108. Find the birthplace of Isadora Duncan, the American-born dancer who died in 1927.

109. Who were the parents of the deceased U.S. corporation executive, Benjamin F. Fairless?

110. Find Dame Margot Fonteyne's birth date.

111. Who was the U.S. Ambassador to France in 1832?

112. What books has Frederick B. Gipson written besides Old Yeller, which has an appeal to children, and would it be possible to find his picture and an illustration from one of his books?

113. Who is Beverly Linney Hallam, an American, who has something to do with art?

114.  Where could you find an article on Joseph Hebert,
      grandson of Canada's first settler?

115.  Where could you find a list of reference books on Ital-
      ian pseudonyms?

116.  Where could one find a fairly long article on Amanda
      Theodosia Jones, an American inventor who died in
      1914?

117.  What essays have been written recently about D. H.
      Lawrence?

118.  Find a list of American Nobel Prize winners.

119.  Who was Thomas Love Peacock?

120.  What was the occupation of Horace H. Rackham, an
      American who lived between 1858 and 1933?

121.  What was the English painter Joseph Farington's sub-
      ject specialty?

122.  Where could you find a signature facsimile of the Amer-
      ican author  Katharine Green Rohlfs?

123.  Find a list of biographical dictionaries in many lan-
      guages dealing with people in library science and the
      book arts.

124.  Where could you find information concerning the back-
      ground of the Canadian manufacturer, William Ian
      Mackenzie Turner?

125.  What is the educational background of the American
      Charles Henry Watts II?

126.  Where can I find a lengthy, signed biography of Wil-
      liam Wordsworth, which includes a list of portraits
      of the poet?

127.  Find an evaluative biography of the late British poet
      A. E. Housman.

128.  Locate an evaluative biography of the Puritan clergy-
      man Cotton Mather.

129. What was the birth date of the late British actor, Ronald Colman?

130. With which important event in American history is Robert Morris (1734-1806) associated?

131. In what area of science were the Shull brothers active?

132. How many children did former President Herbert Hoover have?

133. Find an evaluative biography with a bibliography on Thomas Jefferson.

134. Who was the author of an article on Chaucer appearing in 1956?

135. In what source would you find a list of biographical dictionaries of women artists from the seventh century B. C. to 1970?

136. When did Bret Harte die?

137. How do you pronounce the name Abdullah?

138. What reference source would you consult to find out what Andrew Jackson's mother's maiden name was?

139. What is Frank Sinatra's address?

140. Find biographies of Swedenborgian ministers.

141. In what year was the Ethical Culture Society founded?

142. What is the date of death of Sir Gilbert Hollinshed Bloomfield Jackson, the late Chairman of the Conscientious Objector Appellate Tribunal of England?

143. Where could you look to see if Sir Henry Head was really a neurologist and the editor of Brain?

144. What was Lenin's full name?

145. Locate a list of essays on Alexander Pope.

146. What was the education of Louis Muñoz Marín, a governor of Puerto Rico?

147. What is the date of birth of the late William Gibson, appointed Parliament Secretary in 1937?

148. Who was called the "Father of the American Cotton Industry"?

149. Find the birthplace of John Stark.

150. Find dates for Samuel Allibone, lexicographer and librarian.

151. Who was Louis Swift?

152. Who was Caesar De Missy?

153. What significant contribution did Sir Thomas Lombe (1685-1739) make to the textile industry?

154. Where would you find information on Clarence's relationship to Richard III?

155. Where would you look for the present address of Pierre Salinger?

156. What was the Baron of Fairfield's real name?

157. Where could you easily discover what Sir John Cope did to Bonnie Prince Charles?

158. Where would you look if you wanted to know if John Ciardi, the American, has any sons?

159. Locate a list of articles on Louis Pasteur.

160. Find a list of books by Lloyd Goodrich, the noted museum director.

161. What is the educational background of the Rev. Cuthbert Charles Lattey, the late British theologian?

162. Who was the governor of Rhode Island in 1640?

163. Find a brief statement of Charles Steinmetz' contribution to electrical engineering.

164. Find a biography of Mary Ann Bickerdyke, a nurse during the Civil War.

165. What businessmen have made the news recently?

166. Locate a list of the important films directed by François Truffaut.

167. What reference source would you consult to find out who John Lodge was?

168. Who was Speaker of the House during Van Buren's administration?

169. What was the nationality of David Gregory (1661-1708), a noted mathematician and astronomer?

170. Where can the title of a dictionary of Polish poets be found?

171. Where can be found a list of works by Euripides?

172. How is the Chinese name, Yung Cheng, pronounced?

173. Where can be found a biography of Gaius Lucilius, the Roman satirist?

174. Where can be found a list of people historically associated with the Cape of Good Hope?

175. Where can be found the name of the reigning king of Jordan?

176. Locate a picture of Sean Connery.

177. Find a list of businessmen currently in the news.

178. Find a biography of Ian Smith.

179. Locate a biography and picture of Richard Burton.

180. Find a concise biography of Napoleon Bonaparte.

181. Find the title of a novel written by Giorgio de Chirico, an Italian artist who influenced the surrealists.

182. Locate references to current periodical articles on J. S. Bach.

183. Find a reference to an obituary of Robert Frost.

184.   Find a list of essays about Marcel Proust.

185.   Find a reference to a critical essay about Sinclair
       Lewis' Elmer Gantry.

186.   Find a citation to a biography of Virginia Dare, the
       first child of English parents born in the New World.

187.   Find a critical appraisal of Dostoievski's Crime and
       Punishment.

188.   Find a biography of Andrew Jackson appropriate for
       a child.

189.   Where is Robert Morris, the American Revolutionary
       War financier, buried?

190.   Find a biography of Ernest Hemingway.

191.   Locate a list of past presidents of the University of
       Chicago.

192.   Find a list of the major publications of the anthropolo-
       gist, Ruth Benedict, who lived from 1887 to 1948.

193.   What was the educational background of the entertainer
       Jean Harlow?

194.   What pseudonyms has Marjorie Prebble used?

195.   Does Luis Zalamea have any children?

196.   What awards has David G. Simons received?

197.   Find a picture of Andre Norton, a writer of science
       fiction.

198.   What were the political activities of Benjamin Franklin?

199.   When did King George III die?

200.   What was Woodrow Wilson's occupation before he be-
       came President?

201.   Who are some of the famous people in American history
       who were born in Indiana?

202.  What was Millard Fillmore's birth date?

203.  Find a biography of F. Scott Fitzgerald with a portrait.

204.  Find a list of women abolitionists.

205.  Find an evaluation of Miles Standish.

206.  Locate a description of the childhood of Henry VIII.

207.  What was Charles Marriott's profession?

208.  When was Major Edward Fagan, the late English military officer, born?

209.  When was Lloyd George, the former Prime Minister of England, born?

210.  Find an evaluative biography of Oliver Cromwell.

211.  Where was Howard Hughes born?

212.  Find a lengthy biography of James McNeill Whistler.

213.  Find bibliographical information on a dictionary of French pseudonyms.

214.  What was the death date of Aubrey Beardsley, the English artist?

215.  What is the pronunciation of Fa-Hsien, the fourth-century Chinese priest and author?

216.  Find a discussion of the career of Rabbi Stephen Wise, an early twentieth-century religious leader.

217.  Find a biography and a listing of works of Alexander Pope.

218.  Locate recent periodical articles on Beethoven.

219.  Find the birth and death dates of the American evangelist, Aimee Semple McPherson.

220.  Find a biography with a portrait of Soupy Sales.

221.  Find an account of the projects initiated by Louise

Caldwell Murdock, founder of the Twentieth Century
Club of Wichita, Kansas in 1896.

223.  Find a biography, with a picture, of Carolyn Keene,
      the author of the Nancy Drew books.

224.  Locate an evaluative biography of Peter Roget, a
      nineteenth-century London physician.

225.  Find a biography with a photograph of Neil Armstrong,
      the astronaut.

226.  Find a list of books in which can be found biographical
      articles about Borodin, a nineteenth-century Russian
      composer.

227.  In what magazine did an article about Charles Dickens
      called "Dip into Dickens" appear in 1962?

228.  Find career information on the late Sir J. William
      Dawson, former Principal of McGill University in
      Montreal.

229.  What did Enoch Lincoln, who lived from 1788 to 1892,
      do in American history?

230.  Find a biography of Enrico Dandolo, who lived from
      1108 to 1205.

231.  Find a biography of Joseph Kennedy.

232.  Find a short biography of Ralph W. Gallagher, former
      Chairman of Standard Oil, who died in 1952.

233.  How is the last name of John Gielgud pronounced?

234.  Find a list of Italian biographical dictionaries.

235.  Who was Coriolanus?

236.  What was the date of death of Frederick Stock?

237.  For what poem is the twelfth-century poet Owain Cy-
      veiliog famous?

238.  How is Christopher Columbus' name spelled in Spanish
      and Italian?

239.  Find a list of materials on T. S. Eliot.

240.  How is Pulitzer pronounced?

241.  What was the birthplace of Will Carleton?

242.  What was the first name of Mr. Oswald, who was sent
      to Paris to ascertain the nature of American peace
      terms in 1782?

243.  Who were the candidates in the presidential election in
      1904?

244.  Find a biography of Loretta Young.

245.  Find the title of a biography of W. Hogarth.

246.  Find a scholarly, signed article, with a bibliography
      on Caleb Harris, a nineteenth-century American bib-
      liophile.

247.  Find a list of United States Senators from 1789 to 1937.

248.  Find a biography of the American architect, Samuel
      Inman Cooper.

249.  Find a summary of the stage career of Robert Newton,
      the English actor who died in 1956.

250.  Find the title of a periodical article published in 1974
      about the marriage of King Charles II of England.

251.  Find a signed article on Sir Richard Whitbourne, the
      sixteenth-century English adventurer.

252.  Find an evaluative biography of James Tanner, a de-
      ceased American lobbyist.

253.  Locate an article on the founder of Detroit.

254.  Find an international list of biographical dictionaries
      of musicians.

255.  Find a biography of Louis Untermeyer.

256.  In what reference books would I be able to find biog-
      raphies of Abbas I, Shah of Persia from 1557 to 1628?

257.  In which encyclopedias would I find articles about Jay
      Gould, who lived from 1836 to 1892?

258. Find a biography of Adolph Ochs, publisher of the <u>New York Times</u> from 1896 to 1935, with the correct pronunciation of his name.

259. Where did Robert E. Beard receive the Ph. D. in Slavic linguistics?

260. Where may I find a biography of the actress Patricia Neal?

261. Find a brief biography of Elvis Presley.


## Reference Materials


American Men and Women of Science
Biographical Dictionaries and Related Works
Biography and Genealogy Master Index
Biography Index
Canadian Who's Who
Chambers's Biographical Dictionary
Contemporary Authors
Current Biography
Dictionary of American Biography
Dictionary of Canadian Biography
Dictionary of National Biography
Dictionary of Universal Biography
Directory of American Scholars
Encyclopedia of American Biography
Essay and General Literature Index
Historical Biographical Dictionaries Master Index
International Who's Who
McGraw-Hill Encyclopedia of World Biography
National Cyclopedia of American Biography
Notable American Women
Notable Names in American History
Personal Name Index to the New York Times Index
Something About the Author
Webster's American Biographies
Webster's Biographical Dictionary
Who Was Who
Who Was Who in America
Who's Who
Who's Who in America
Who's Who in the World
Who's Who of American Women

# CHAPTER 5

## BIBLIOGRAPHY AND LIBRARY SCIENCE

### Reference Interviews

Patron #1.  A man.

Patron:     Do you have a list of Andrew Lang's colored
            books?
Librarian:  Did you want just those in print now?
Patron:     Yes.

            Where would you look?


Patron #2.  A high school girl.

Patron:     I'd like to find out the definition of "bolt."
Library:    Did you check our unabridged dictionary?
Patron:     No--but this has to do with books.  I think it
            might be a part of a book.

            Where would you find book trade terms?


Patron #3.  A woman.

Patron:     How do I find out if a book is still in print?
Librarian:  What information do you have about the book--
            author, title?
Patron:     It's The Spy by James Fenimore Cooper.

            Where could you find this information?

Patron #4.    A young woman.

Patron:        I want to know if this book, Rape of the Fair Coun-
               try, is still in print and who the publisher is
               now.   It's British.   I've already checked Books
               in Print and it's not there.
Librarian:     Who is the author?
Patron:        Alexander Cordell.
Librarian:     According to CBI Alexander Cordell is a pseu-
               donym.

               Where would you go now?


Patron #5.    A man.

Patron:        I really have a problem and I don't think you
               can help me but you're my last resort.
Librarian:     What's the problem?
Patron:        My wife saw a book a few months ago that she
               said she wanted.   I'd like to order it for her
               for Christmas, but I can't remember the author
               or title.
Librarian:     Do you know what the book is about?
Patron:        Yes, it's an art book.
Librarian:     Do you know if it was about the art of a certain
               period or country?
Patron:        Well, I think it was about the history of Mexican
               art and as I remember, it was quite expensive--
               around $25 or $30.

               Where would you check?


Patron #6.    A high school student.

Patron:        I need some books of historical fiction.
Librarian:     Historical fiction of what country?
Patron:        United States.
Librarian:     Any particular period?
Patron:        Around the Revolutionary War.

               Where could you find a list of suitable novels?


Patron #7.    A woman.

Patron:     I'm interested in the poems of Phillis Wheatley.
Librarian:  You'd like to read some of her poems?
Patron:     Yes.
Librarian:  Granger's Index of Poetry only lists four of her
            poems.  We might have one or two of them in
            an anthology; or did you want an entire book of
            her poems?
Patron:     I'd prefer a book if there is one.

            Where would you look?


Patron #8.  A woman.

Patron:     I would like to see a list of fiction books.
Librarian:  There is a list of current best-sellers at the
            check-out desk.  Is that what you want?
Patron:     No, I'd like a longer list, maybe with some
            critical remarks.

            Where would you look?


Patron #9.  A man.

Patron:     I'd like to find out something about Oriental
            games--Japanese or Chinese chess.
Librarian:  (Looking in Subject Guide to BIP)  There are
            two listed here.
Patron:     I wanted to buy one or two books, so I'd prefer
            something in paperback.

            Where would you go?


Patron #10.  A high school boy.

Patron:     Do you have any war stories?
Librarian:  About any special war?
Patron:     Yes, World War II.
Librarian:  Are you interested in fiction or non-fiction?
Patron:     Fiction.

            Where would you check?

## Reference Questions

1. How would you locate a library within the United States which has a special collection on Beethoven? Where is it?

2. Explain what is meant by a "Bowdlerized text."

3. Who publishes an in-print English-Vietnamese dictionary?

4. In a comprehensive manual on style, on what page will you find the principal and guide meridians and baselines of the U.S.? How many inches are equal to 125 picas?

5. Does Allen Ginsberg have a collection of poems available in paperback?

6. Define the following abbreviations from the book trade: ABA, Bds, Col (d), P.P., T.L.s.

7. Find a definition of "corner clip." What is the Spanish equivalent of this term?

8. What is the translation of "proofreading" into Spanish?

9. What do the initials I.D.P. stand for?

10. Locate the cost of two travel guides to Rome with brief annotations.

11. What are the LC card numbers of some books on differential geometry for college students? (pre-1964)

12. Find three phonorecords of Irish folk dance music.

13. Who was the co-author with Patrick O'Reilly of Jaunes, Noirs et Blancs, Paris, 1949? What is the LC number?

14. Find three books for a 5th grader who wants to learn about puppetry.

15. Who was the writer of A Million Years of Man, an NBC News film released in 1967?

16. Is LC the only library which holds American New Life, v. 1-, 1901-?

17.  Who published Joe Louis' autobiography?

18.  What is the title of a work by John Champneys printed in London in 1548?

19.  What U.S. libraries hold the Institute of Makers of Explosives pamphlet no. 17, 1960?

20.  Where could one find an annotated list of books about U.S. foreign policy which are recommended for high school students?

21.  Which library has a master microfilm of John Wesley's A Short English Grammar?

22.  What does the term, "agate," which is used in connection with book binding, mean?

23.  What U.S. library has a copy of David Raymond Cheney's Animals in a Midsummer Night's Dream, which was written in 1955?

24.  What is the address of the Antiquarian Booksellers' Association?

25.  Find the French and Spanish terms for "bookworm."

26.  What are some synonyms for "half-title" as used in library science?

27.  What is the title of a book on chess suitable for children?

28.  Locate a select bibliography on aluminum which provides annotations.

29.  Where could one find the names of some pamphlets on Yugoslavia?

30.  What is the approximate market value of a first edition of Twain's Huckleberry Finn?

31.  What is the title of the book that Margaret Truman Daniels wrote in 1969?

32.  What did Lady Marie Thérèse Louise Dickens publish in 1936?

33. Can you suggest an in-print book on "Family Allowances"?

34. Who has been called the "Father of Modern Painting"?

35. What are the titles of some books on the floral arts which are appropriate for a public library?

36. What does the Czech word, "bukinista," mean?

37. What are some of the more significant recent developments in the area of information science?

38. What is the title of the book Marion Levy wrote on China in 1949?

39. Find an article on libraries in Afghanistan.

40. Find recent statistics on the educational status of library users in the U.S.

41. Find a few paragraphs defining the term, "limited edition."

42. Find a bibliography of Iris Murdoch's works along with a short, critical biography of her and a list of works about her.

43. Who is the law librarian for the New Mexico Supreme Court?

44. Who really wrote "How I won over fifty prizes in weekly periodicals," a work originally signed with the initials "J. E. S."?

45. What are the major emphases in the Grosvenor Library's rare book collection?

46. How would you say "reference department" in six languages?

47. Find a bibliography of journal articles written between 1883 and 1917 concerned with the classification of materials in the subject of religion.

48. Has anyone published a bibliography of graduate theses and dissertations about the American Indian?

49. Who wrote <u>Analysis of the Game of Chess</u>, published in London in 1819?

50. What is the French equivalent for the term, "short-title"?

51. Has anyone published a bibliography of the works of Adam Smith?

52. Find an excerpt from a review of Edna Ferber's book <u>So Big</u>.

53. Which special libraries are located in Princeton, New Jersey?

54. What is the mailing address of the librarian Elizabeth Stone?

55. What is the Library of Congress number of <u>Time as Dimension and History</u> by Hubert Griggs Alexander, published by the University of Mexico Press in 1945?

56. What does the Swedish work, "bibliografisk," mean?

57. How would one say "xerography" in Bulgarian?

58. What is the book budget at the University of Alaska Library?

59. What is the name of a Venezuelan bibliography on education?

60. What is the educational background of the librarian Robert Coale?

61. Find an evaluation of the past year's work on the design of information systems.

62. Locate the real author of <u>Mabel</u> written under the pseudonym, Grace Ramsay.

63. Find the approximate value of a first edition of Dickens' <u>Mystery of Edwin Drood</u>.

64. What is the meaning of the Italian book term, "pagine"?

65. What are the titles of some recent bibliographies published on the subject of "demography"?

66. What are the correct uses of italics in preparing a work for printing?

67. What are some books on the subject of "kindergarten"?

68. I have just received the proofs for my book from the publisher.   What do I do with them now?

69. What other work has the author of <u>Discipline</u>, published in Edinburgh in 1814, written?

70. If someone described a book to you as "grossissimo," where would you find out what that means?

71. What doctoral dissertation has been written on the novels of Robert Bage?

72. I have a new job as a proofreader for the college paper. What will be some of my responsibilities?

73. Where would one find out the meaning of "elite type"?

74. Does the U. S. army maintain a library in Munich?

75. What are the anonymous publications of President James Madison?

76. Where may I find a copy of the letter written by Columbus after he discovered America?

77. Where might one find out whether or not the New York Times Photo Library is open to the public?

78. Is there a library in the U. S. where I can find some special material on the Mennonites?

79. Where would you locate a selection of books on religion suitable for an academic library which covers a variety of different viewpoints on numerous aspects of the subject?

80. How many degrees were awarded in library science last year?

81. Under what two pseudonyms did Eliza Louisa Moresby Beck publish her novel and short stories in the 1930s?

82. List the single works of Rudyard Kipling.

83. Where might one go to find out what is on the other
    side of a recording by William Primrose of Hindemith's
    Der Schwanendreher issued with the L. C. card #R54-
    812?

84. Where can I find a list of books on twentieth-century
    music?

85. Where might one find the name of the head librarian
    of the Vermont Historical Society Library?

86. Where could one find the title of a book to study to pre-
    pare for the Civil Service Exam for elevator inspectors?

87. How many new books were published in the field of fiction
    in the U. S. last year?

88. Where might one find a list of books on communism in
    the U. S. for which L. C. cards were issued last year?

89. Where might one go to find a list of Bulgarian fiction
    books that were assigned L. C. cards last year?

90. Where might one find the imprint of the original print-
    ing of Walt Whitman's November Boughs?

91. What are some good books suggesting chemical experi-
    ments for third grade children?

92. Which auction house sold a first edition of R. L. Ste-
    venson's Child's Garden of Verses in 1895?

93. Is there a book written about the First Ladies of the
    U. S. ?

94. What would be some good books to use as the nucleus
    of a new undergraduate library?

95. Where would you locate a recommended biography of
    Henry of Navarre, King of France?

96. Was Treasure Island sold in first edition in 1894 at an
    American auction?

97. Where might one go to find out who wrote the music for

the 1955 film, The Rose Tattoo, starring Anna Mag-
nani and Burt Lancaster?

98.  Where would one find the name of the publisher and
cost of the book Chitty-chitty-bang-bang by Ian Flem-
ing?

99.  Locate the titles of several currently published books
dealing with African writers.

100. What does the word "stereotype" mean in its original
sense?  It has something to do with printing.

101. Where would you find recent dissertations in the field
of literature?

102. Where might one find a list of libraries in the country
that have Charles Guthrie's book, Blood Vessel Surgery
and Its Applications (1959)?

103. Locate the titles of some current dictionaries dealing
with cookery.

104. Where would one find the birth date of the famous
bookman, Elmer Adler?

105. What are the names of some libraries in Oslo, Norway?

106. Where might one find the Library of Congress number
for Middlesex, a 1951 book by Norman Brett-James?

107. Where can I find an account of English book illustration in the early 1900s, written by a contemporary of
the period?

108. Which publishers are still printing copies of William
Faulkner's Light in August?  Are any paperback editions currently available?

109. Where might one go to find out the plot of a 1953 film,
The Robe, and if Richard Burton starred in it or not?

110. What price was paid in 1895 for an autographed letter
signed by Charles Baudelaire to his publisher in which
Victor Hugo and Théophile Gautier were mentioned?

111. Is there an English translation of Sartre's play Les
     Sèquestres d'Altona?

112. Where might one find out the size of a book called
     Who's to Blame by Henry Fauntleroy, printed in 1883?

113. Where would one go to find fairly complete reproduc-
     tions of L. C. cards if one were preparing a bibliog-
     raphy in the field of organic chemistry?

114. Where might one find a number of books on antibiotics
     published recently?

115. What kind of book activities are carried on by the
     Agency for International Development?

116. Is there a library in New York that has a special col-
     lection on Mary, Queen of Scots?

117. Where might one find the type of holdings of the Chem-
     strand Corp. Technical Library?

118. Where can one find the meaning of the abbreviation
     "cf. ," a term used in a footnote or bibliography?

119. Who is the author of Adventures of an Irish Gentleman,
     published anonymously in London in 1830?

120. Where might one find the L. C. card number for a set
     of the complete works of Brahms printed by J. W.
     Edwards in 1949?

121. Are any editions of the Holy Quran currently available
     which provide both the Arabic text and an English
     translation?

122. Who were the authors of an 1899 British work on hockey?

123. Locate information regarding current developments
     concerning the Copyright Office of the Library of Con-
     gress for the previous year.

124. Locate the translation of the French word, "rayonnage,"
     into English.

125. What is the German word for "foliated"?

126.    What is oversewing?

127.    What are the dimensions of a sexto-decimo edition?

128.    What is the difference between the words "serials" and "series"?

129.    Locate information on John Baskerville, the English printer.

130.    Does the University of Alberta Press have a book in print on the history of Boeotia?

131.    What is the meaning of "rubricated"?

132.    What is the meaning of "offprint"?

133.    What are "incunabula"?

134.    For what does "C. & P." stand?

135.    Identify the term, "Chiswick Press."

136.    Find an explanation of MARC tapes, which are used by many libraries.

137.    What is "flexible classification"?

138.    What is the meaning of the Dutch book term, "vellen"?

139.    Who was Pierre Simon Fournier?

140.    How is "publisher's catalog" translated into German?

141.    Locate a list of publications of the American Society for Information Science for the previous year.

142.    How many bibliographies on St. John Chrysostom have been prepared by Dom Baur?

143.    What does the proofreading mark, #, mean?

144.    Find rules for the use of italics in printing.

145.    Locate a list of works distinguished as the "Best Children's Books" of the previous year. How are these books selected and by what group?

146. Have any libraries in the Decatur, Illinois area been designated as U. S. government depositories?

147. What type of bookmobile services are offered by the Toronto Public Library (Canada)?

148. How does one make footnote references to legal documents?

149. What is the format for compiling a list of tables to be included in a dissertation?

150. Locate rules for dividing words at the ends of lines.

151. How does one make a bibliography of illustrations?

152. What is the proper cover form for a brief for the Supreme Court?

153. Which colleges and universities in New York offer graduate programs in library science?

154. What is the correct right-hand margin to be used in typing a thesis?

155. Find the name of a bibliography of Coptic literature printed in Russian.

156. Find a bibliography about Japanese theatre and drama.

157. Find a reference to a recent bibliography listing military books.

158. Locate recent bibliographies about information storage and retrieval systems.

159. Find the title of a Dutch bibliography of Javanese literature.

160. Find the condition and approximate value of a map of Mexico by J. Hutawa, produced in 1863.

161. Which auction house sold a 1696 Dutch translation of Don Quixote?

162. What was the auction price, at the most recent sale, of a first edition of Blackstone's Commentaries on the Laws of England?

163.  Find a list of books of ghost stories for children.

164.  Have any of Yukio Misima's works been translated into English?

165.  What is Kate Norway's real name?

166.  Where may be found information on discounts from publishers to book stores?

167.  Are there any books in print about Adolf Eichmann, the former Nazi?

168.  Are any of B. F. Skinner's books available in paper bindings?

169.  Are there any paperback books on training beagles?

170.  What significance does the term "diaper" have for the book trade and library profession?

171.  What is a more common term for "duodecimo"?

172.  How many sheets does a ream of paper contain and how would you communicate the answer to a German-speaking person?

173.  For what specialized bookbinding techniques are the Edwards family of Halifax remembered?

174.  What is the correct format for citing congressional bills and resolutions before they have been enacted?

175.  Find a brief account of the library system of a state prison in Denmark.

176.  From which institution can a microfilmed copy of the Book of Mormon be obtained?

177.  Is Putnam's Magazine available in microform?

178.  How much does Gone with the Wind cost in paperback?

179.  Find a brief description of the New England Document Conservation Center.

180.  Who publishes Fraser's Canadian Trade Directory in Canada?

181.  Where is the master microform from which copies of
      Lang's Modern Mythology may be ordered?

182.  Locate a table giving the recommended metric sizes
      for books.

183.  How much does a copy of The Adventures of Pinocchio
      cost?

184.  Where could one find the title of a thesis written on
      the Brontës?

185.  Where could one find a list of pamphlets on drug abuse?

186.  Where could one find an annotated list of travel guides
      to foreign countries?

187.  Did the Library Journal give Heyerdahl's Aku-Aku a
      favorable review?

188.  Find a synopsis of Robert Bolt's play, A Man for All
      Seasons.

189.  Find a list of atlases and maps useful in a public li-
      brary.

190.  Locate the title of a good book about ballet for fifth
      grade children.

191.  In which anthologies can a fairy tale entitled "The
      Jolly Tailor Who Became King" be located?

192.  What are some synonymous terms for "variorum edi-
      tion," used by U.S. publishers?

193.  Find a list of psychological novels.

194.  Who was the original publisher of J. R. R. Tolkien's
      Lord of the Rings trilogy?

195.  Is Victoria Holt's novel, The Legend of the Seventh
      Virgin, suitable for teenagers?

196.  What are some good college level books in the field
      of plant physiology?

197.  Who published Bertolt Brecht's Mutter Courage und
      Ihre Kinder?

80                                    Interviews and Questions

198.    Find a brief biographical sketch of Dante Gabriel Ros-
        setti, the Italian poet.

199.    How much does John Berryman's 77 Dream Songs cost
        and which publisher puts it out?

200.    Which editions of Shakespeare's works are available
        in paperback?

201.    Find an annotated, evaluative list of books on word
        usage.

202.    Is John Kenneth Galbraith's Economic Development in
        Perspective recommended for public libraries?

203.    Find the full order information and quotations from
        critics on Waiting for Godot by Samuel Beckett.

204.    Find a list of biographies about black people suitable
        for teenagers.

205.    Would Veronica's Smile by Roger Duvoisin or A Dog
        So Small by Philippa Pearce be better for a six-year-
        old?

206.    From where could a pamphlet on venereal disease be
        ordered?

207.    What are the nicknames of Martin Bormann, the Ger-
        man Nazi party leader?

208.    What do the initials stand for in J. R. R. Tolkien's
        name?

209.    Who was the "First American Negro Novelist"?

210.    Should the "S" in Harry S Truman's name have a period
        after it?

211.    Find a list of articles written in the first decade of
        this century about librarianship as a career for women.

212.    Find the names of some prominent journals in librarian-
        ship at the turn of the century.

213.    Find summaries of recent works on the application of
        computers to librarianship.

214. Find evaluative remarks on recent books in the field of information science.

215. Locate a summary account of the damage sustained by libraries in Florence during the November, 1966, floods.

216. Find an illustrated article on ancient libraries.

217. Locate a biographical sketch of Vasilii Anastasevich, an early nineteenth-century Russian.

218. What is the name of the librarian at the University of Toronto?

219. A doctoral student in English literature is writing a dissertation on Herman Melville. Which library in the U. S. has the most comprehensive collection of materials by and about this author suitable for an exhaustive study?

220. What is the pseudonym of Alfred du Pont?

221. Locate the address of your state library association.

222. Which organization gave the most grant money to libraries in the United States last year?

223. Find a list of associations especially interested in the automation of libraries.

224. Find a list of officers of the Canadian Library Association.

225. What is the total public library circulation for Illinois?

226. What are the locations of U. S. I. A. libraries in Europe?

227. How many volumes are in the New York Public Library?

228. What types of special materials on Frank Lloyd Wright does the Northwestern University Library have in its collection?

229. In which New York serial was Nathaniel Hawthorne's story "The Snow Image" first published?

230.  Where could one find a bibliography of the works of
      Jonathan Edwards.

231.  Where could one find the title of an unpublished thesis
      by Albert Díaz about the Latin American collection in
      the University of North Carolina library?

232.  What kinds of material on music history are to be
      found in the Detroit Public Library's Music and Per-
      forming Arts Department?

233.  Locate a list of libraries which have special collections
      of rare books.

234.  Was there ever an edition published of The Castle by
      Franz Kafka which contained an introduction by Thomas
      Mann?

235.  Find the address of the General Electric Company Com-
      puter Department Library.

236.  What are some of the special collections of the J. M.
      Longyear Research Library of the Marquette County
      (Michigan) Historical Society?

237.  What is the size of the Kimball Public Library in Ran-
      dolph, Vermont?

238.  Find a list of the early editions and manuscripts of
      Thomas Paine held in the Clements Library of the Uni-
      versity of Michigan.

239.  Find a list of United States regional libraries for the
      blind.

240.  What are requirements for membership in the American
      Theological Library Association?

241.  Find a biographical description of an 1872 edition of
      Thomas Hardy's book, Under the Greenwood Tree.

242.  Find full bibliographical information for The National
      Guardsman, a journal published from 1877 to 1878.

243.  What is the 1952 movie, "Toughest Man in Arizona,"
      about?

244. Find full bibliographical information for a book published in 1941 by a man named Otto Gliss.

245. What did Edith Abbott Fritten, who died in 1957, write in her lifetime?

246. Find bibliographical information on a map of Capitola, California, printed in 1949.

247. Find bibliographical information about the libretto of Camelot, a musical comedy copyrighted in 1961.

248. Find a listing of children's books about medicine.

249. Has "The Five Chinese Brothers" been made into a filmstrip?

250. What is the movie, "Che Heroes," about?

251. Are there any movies explaining the germination of seeds?

252. Find a list of recordings of Norwegian folksongs.

253. Find a listing of musical compositions by Eugene Goossens.

254. Find a reference to excerpts from "West Side Story" arranged for piano and voice.

255. Who translated an 1817 edition of the complete Bible into Chinese?

256. Who was the publisher of an edition of Dante's The Purgatorio which provided an Italian and English version on opposite pages?

257. Did the Library of Congress catalog any books about the Hittite language from July through September, 1967?

258. Who was the publisher of Benjamin Musser's Bucolics and Caviar, which came out in 1930?

259. Find the Library of Congress number, the translator, and a list of libraries holding a copy of Natalia Ginzburg's A Light for Fools, published in 1956.

260.  Locate a list of Christmas stories available on film-
      strips.

261.  Has the Library of Congress cataloged any of the Beatles'
      albums?

262.  Are there any American libraries which have copies
      of Claude Amiette's Peine Perdue, which was published
      in 1955?

263.  During which years was La Revue Blanche, a Parisian
      periodical, published?

264.  Find a list of critical and biographical works about
      the Marquis de Sade written in several different lang-
      uages.

265.  From which source can one order copies printed from
      a master microfilm of the New Jersey Journal of Phar-
      macy?

266.  Are there any paperback books about computer-assisted
      instruction for sale?

267.  Find the name of one of the French-to-English trans-
      lations of a Georges Simenon novel published outside
      the United States.

268.  Who was the author of the anonymous play, "The Maca-
      roni," which was first presented in 1773 in York, Eng-
      land?

269.  Find a summary of a 1968 doctoral thesis on the Han
      Dynasty in China.

270.  Find a list of separately collated bibliographies on chil-
      dren's literature with an international scope.

271.  Find a title of a 1967 bibliography on Victorian jewelry.

272.  What call number was assigned to Peter Prim's Story
      Book by the Library of Congress?

273.  Is The Red Badge of Courage available in a large type
      edition?

274.  Find the Library of Congress number for a Hebrew
      literature bibliography published in 1957.

275. Locate a list of good books about reptiles for high school students.

276. Find a book about the Chinese language which is suitable for an elementary school child.

277. Which record company has a 1968 recording of Puccini's "La Bohème"?

278. Find the average price of a book published last year.

279. What is the name of the director of the University of North Carolina libraries?

280. Find the auction price of Ballad Books, edited by C. K. Sharpe and published in 1823.

281. What is the meaning of the term, "herdrukt," discovered in a Dutch bibliography?

282. What is a "library edition"?

283. If one needed a copy of Cornelius Baldwin's Ancient Burial Cists in Northern Ohio, which was published in 1882, where is the closest library holding a copy?

284. Does the University of Minnesota Press have any titles on home economics for sale?

285. Find annotations for children's books written by David C. Cooke.

286. What is the German equivalent of the English term, "classified arrangement"?

287. Find a list of the books about Musa Kaago which have been published in English in the twentieth century.

288. What does "unlettered" mean to the antiquarian bookman?

289. Find a list of paperback books about Franklin D. Roosevelt.

290. Find a summary of Sidney Mitchell's 1963 doctoral thesis on Joseph Conrad.

291. What is the address of the Science Fiction Book Club?

292.   Find bibliographical data on a 1905 article on college
       libraries in Oregon.

293.   Find an explanation of an extension card in library
       practice.

294.   Were there any French bibliographies on the topic of
       hypnotism published before 1900?

295.   Locate an essay on the history of French literature
       which includes a bibliography listing the current prices
       of the books.

296.   What awards has Carl Sandburg received?

297.   Which libraries have the Baltimore Philosophical Journal
       on microfilm?

298.   What is the address of the publisher of the Book of
       Knowledge?

299.   What is the address of the Barrows Publishing Com-
       pany?

300.   What are the titles of some novels about New York
       City?

301.   What is the address of Scribner's?

302.   What is the address of the publisher, Stratford House?

303.   What is the address of McGraw-Hill?

304.   What is the title of a novel about music or musicians?

305.   What is the address of the National Education Associa-
       tion?

306.   What is the address of Funk and Wagnalls?

307.   Find a list of books on Napoleon.

308.   Find a list of books on pyrometers.

309.   Locate a list of novels about early English history.

310.   Are there any novels about Valley Forge?

311. Can you recommend a good novel about the Civil War in the United States?

312. Are there any novels about the wives of Henry VIII?

313. Are there any novels about South Africa?

314. What are the names of special libraries in Alabama having Civil War collections?

315. Who is the director of libraries at Case Western Reserve University?

316. What is the price of the Reader's Encyclopedia?

317. Find a list of books on ballet.

318. Find an essay having to do with library architecture.

319. What is a book scout?

320. When did John Bell, the English bookseller, printer, and publisher live?

321. What were the major activities of the Catholic Library Association last year?

322. What does the Czech phrase, "osli ucho," having to do with books, mean?

323. What is a "double entry" in library work?

324. In what periodical did an article by L. B. Evans entitled "What the Library Can Do for the Boy," published in 1911, appear?

325. What are the correct uses of italics in preparing a work for printing?

326. What did a first edition of Rudyard Kipling's Just So Stories for Little Children sell for in London in 1964?

327. In what periodical did Hattie M. Knight's article, "Library Education: a More Excellent Way," appear in the fall of 1969?

328. What was the name of the periodical in which an article on lighting for public libraries appeared in 1897?

329.  What books on the subject of lizards are currently for
      sale in the United States?

330.  What special libraries are located in New Brunswick,
      New Jersey?

331.  Who is the author of the novel, At Home, which on the
      title page says that it is by the "author of English
      Fashionables Abroad"?

332.  What book by John D. Ryder did the Library of Cong-
      ress acquire in 1949?

333.  What is the symbol, ... , called and what is the Rus-
      sian equivalent?

334.  Locate a list of biographies of George Washington, with
      annotations, suitable for children and recommended
      by the American Library Association.

335.  Find a list of microfilm masters, with libraries which
      hold them, for the works of Washington Irving.

336.  Which United States libraries have copies of James
      Thomas Field's Good Company for Every Day in the
      Year, published in 1866?

337.  Has the city of Adlington in Lancashire, England, pub-
      lished an official city guide since 1956?

338.  What is a "llyfrigellyd"?

339.  What children's books are available for sale on the
      subject of monsters?

340.  What are the titles in the series Concise Medical Text-
      books?

341.  What is the price of Les Miserables by Victor Hugo,
      for use as a textbook in a secondary school?

342.  What was the native country of Maria Augusta Trapp?

343.  What was George Orwell's real name?

344.  What is the address of the Nepal National Library?

345. Is there an edition of Odessa File by Frederick Forsyth available in a format appropriate for the visually handicapped?

346. What is the address of the Brazilian Association of Librarians?

347. For what does BCM stand?


## Reference Materials

ABC for Book-Collectors
A. L. A. Glossary of Library and Information Science
A. L. A. Membership Directory
American Book-Prices Current
American Library Directory
American Library Resources
American National Standards for Bibliographic References
Annual Review of Information Science and Technology
Associations' Publications in Print
Bibliographic Index
Bibliography of Library Economy
Bookman's Glossary
Bookman's Price Index
Books for College Libraries
Books in Print
Books in Series
Bowker Annual of Library and Book Trade Information
British Books in Print
British Museum.  General Catalogue of Printed Books
British Museum.  Subject Index of the Modern Works Added
  to the Library
Children's Books in Print
Children's Catalog
Comprehensive Dissertation Index
Cumulative Book Index
Dictionaries of Anonymous and Pseudonymous English Literature
Dictionary Catalog of the Arthur Schomburg Collection of
  Negro Literature and History
Dictionary Catalog of the Jesse Moorland Collection of Negro
  Life and History
Dictionary Catalog of the Negro Collection of the Fisk University Library

Dictionary of Literary Pseudonyms
Directory of Special Libraries
Dissertation Abstracts International
El-Hi Textbooks in Print
Elsevier's Dictionary of Library Science, Information and
    Documentation
Encyclopedia of Library and Information Science
Fiction Catalog
Forthcoming Books
Government Printing Office Style Manual
Handbook of Pseudonyms and Personal Nicknames
Information Science Abstracts
International Directory of Acronyms in Library, Information
    and Computer Science
International Guide to Library, Archival, and Information
    Science Associations
Junior High School Library Catalog
The Language of the Foreign Book Trade
Large Type Books in Print
Librarian's Glossary
The Librarian's Practical Dictionary in Twenty-Two Languages
Library and Information Science Abstracts
Library Literature
Library of Congress. Catalog. Books: Subjects
Library Resources Marketplace
A Manual for Writers of Term Papers, Theses and Disserta-
    tions
Manual of European Languages for Librarians
Manual of Style
National Register of Microform Masters
The National Union Catalog
National Union Catalog, Pre-1956 Imprints
Paperbound Books in Print
Pseudonyms and Nicknames
Public Library Catalog
The Publisher's Practical Dictionary in 20 Languages
Publishers' Trade List Annual
The Reader's Adviser
Senior High School Library Catalog
Subject Collections
Subject Guide to Books in Print
Subject Guide to Children's Books in Print
Vertical File Index
Vocabularium Bibliothecarii, English, French, German, Rus-
    sian
Who's Who in Library and Information Science
A World Bibliography of Bibliographies
World Guide to Libraries

CHAPTER 6

## DICTIONARIES

### Reference Interviews

Patron #1.    A junior high school girl.

Patron:        Do you have any books on how to write papers?
Librarian:    Did you want something on how to write the paper
              or how to type it for handing in?
Patron:        No, something on words in papers.
Librarian:    Do you mean synonyms for words?
Patron:        I guess so.  What I want is to find some other
              words that mean the same thing as my words
              but sound better.

              Where would you go?


Patron #2.    A man.

Patron:        I hate to bother you, but I'm helping my daughter
              do her homework and I need help.  Have you
              ever heard of acronyms?
Librarian:    Yes, I have.
Patron:        Well, this dumb teacher has assigned these kids
              to find out what AFRA and ASHA mean and I've
              looked and can't find it.  We have a big un-
              abridged dictionary and it's not even in there.
              Do you think that you could possibly find it?

              Where could you find the answers?


Patron #3.    A little boy.

Patron:       Is decomposer the same as decompose?
Librarian:    Are you trying to decide how to use it?
Patron:       I guess.
Librarian:    Is this for a class?
Patron:       It's for science.

              Where would you look?


## Reference Questions

1.  What is the difference between amoral, immoral, and unmoral?

2.  What does Calapooya mean?

3.  What does the term "cold water" mean?  Why was President Hayes's administration called the "cold water regime"?

4.  Jimmy Durante:  "What I don't dig over there is the British money."  Is the use of "dig" slang?

5.  Distinguish among fearful, awful, dreadful, and frightful.

6.  What is a "flyblister"?

7.  When did fractional currency appear?

8.  What is the meaning of "dittay"?  Give several alternative spellings of the word.

9.  What is the plural of gallows?  When was it first used to mean suspenders?

10. What is the meaning of "ha-ha" in the following quotation?  "The ha! ha! is digging."

11. What is the pronunciation of Hawarden?

12. Find four antonyms for indifference.

13. What are the differences among infer, deduce, and conclude?

14. "J'y suis, j'y reste." Who said it and how is it pronounced?

15. Is "lingulate" derived from a Latin word?

16. Give some antonyms for loquacity.

17. What does "malo mori quam foedari" stand for?

18. What is a moot hall? When was the term first used? What is a mazer? A peel tower?

19. What is a musaraigne?

20. When was the term "oak openings" first used?

21. What is the distinction between noticeable and remarkable?

22. Was the word "outwit" in use before 1800?

23. Is the term "over and above" a cliché?

24. What is a packetarian?

25. What is the size of a paca?

26. AP, May 10, 1951 reported: "The jockey is in the panic rack and ready to go." What is a panic rack?

27. What is a Rahdaree?

28. What is razzamatazz?

29. What is the difference between reoccurence and recurrence?

30. What is a rob-pot?

31. What is the meaning of "rocked in a stone kitchen"?

32. What was the Treaty of San Stefano?

33. What is a sangar?

34. Who first used sequoia as a name for a genus of trees?

35.  Was the word "soused" in use in seventeenth-century England?

36.  What is the name of the male swan?   the female swan?

37.  What are some antonyms for "taciturnity"?

38.  What is the meaning of tire in the following quotation:
     Well-drilled urchins, each behind his tire
     Waited in ranks the wished command to fire.

39.  Was the word "tittle-tattle" in use in England in the 17th century?

40.  Who coined the word "tularemia"?

41.  What is the English meaning of the French word "arbre"?

42.  Where can I find a definition of a "close helmet" with a picture of one?

43.  What is a "giggle-mug"?

44.  What is the distinction between the words "honorable" and "honorary"?

45.  What is the difference between "mantle" and "mantel"?

46.  How did the word "nepotism" originate?

47.  What does the term "nolo contendere" mean?

48.  What is the meaning of the expression, "on the lam"?

49.  What does "paraffin" mean when applied to Cockney people's appearance?

50.  What was the origin of the expression, "border ruffian"?

51.  I want the German word for "salt" with its correct use in several idioms.

52.  What is the proper form of address for use with a United States senator?

53.  What is the Spanish word for "shamrock"?

54. I need a definition of the word "stethoscope," with a small picture of one.

55. Find a list of synonyms for the word "strict."

56. What is a Saratoga trunk?

57. What are several nouns that might be used instead of the word "vulgarity"?

58. Find an illustration of egg-and-dart molding.

59. Please find the etymology of the word "mutton," with quotations illustrating its usage since 1290 A. D.

60. I would like the definition of the French word "Fier," with some literary quotations showing its usage.

61. What does the phrase "Queen Anne is dead" imply?

62. Find an etymology in German of the word "wissenschaftlich."

63. Is Mexico spelled the same way in English as in Spanish?

64. Is an armed truck transferring money from a place of business to a bank called an "armored cow"?

65. What is nystatin?

66. What words are derived from "cameloter"?

67. What are some German synonyms for "interior"?

68. What is the International Civil Aircraft Marking for Switzerland?

69. What is the proper way to address a duke's daughter?

70. How is the German name "Rahel" translated?

71. What is the meaning of Anschluss?

72. What is the origin of the word "check" in reference to checks and balances?

73. Were the terms "ale" and "beer" originally used syn-
    onymously?

74. Is Pago Pago pronounced pay-GO pay-GO?

75. What is the difference between the American and British
    usage of the words "vacation" and "holiday"?

76. What is the meaning of the expression, "Water under
    the bridge"?

77. What are several synonymous phrases for "To give a
    Roland for an Oliver"?

78. What is the meaning of "au gratin"?

79. How long is the Mississippi River?

80. What does the acronym ALCOA stand for?

81. I want to know the German word for "interclavicle."

82. Where can I find the name of the person who said,
    "Rome est dans notre camp et notre camp dans Rome"?

83. How do you say the English word "faugh" in French?

84. What is the English equivalent of the Spanish verb "com-
    er"?

85. How did the meaning of the German word "armut"
    change over the years?

86. Where would you look in order to find the origin of the
    word "anatocism"?

87. What is an antonym for "crawl"?

88. Find a listing of philosophers.

89. What is the meaning of the word "groovy"?

90. What were the main forms of "to have" in Old English?

91. Find the source of an 1889 quotation showing Rider
    Haggard's use of the word "scrawl."

92. What is an antonym for the word "feeling"?

93. Find a photograph illustrating the definition of the word "robin."

94. What is the FHA?

95. What is the French word for "war"?

96. Locate line drawings to illustrate the term "fever-few plant."

97. What is sunshine cake and where can you find a recipe for it?

98. What does a lyre look like?

99. What does "to make the scene" mean?

100. What were the origins of the term "apple-fritter"?

101. What is the earliest written record of the use of the American word "chaparral"?

102. Do "dobie" and "adobe" have different meanings?

103. Find a list of expressions which include the word "boot," and when they originated in the United States.

104. Locate a picture of a lowboy.

105. What is the meaning of the term "sugar daddy"?

106. What does the expression "bring home the bacon" mean?

107. What is the meaning of "ogfray"?

108. What are the differences in the meanings of the terms "intend" and "mean"?

109. Find an antonym for the word "meager."

110. What is the difference in meaning between "connote" and "denote"?

111. Find a list of synonyms for the word "happy."

112.   What does the expression "armored cow" mean?

113.   What were the origins of the expression "cracker bar-rel"?

114.   Locate antonyms and analogous words for the word "surprised."

115.   Is "fiord" or "fjord" the correct English spelling?

116.   Find a discussion and examples of the uses and abuses of inversion in writing.

117.   What is the meaning of the expression, "to shed light upon the subject"?

118.   What is the difference between the British and the American usage of the word "trunk"?

119.   Compare the meanings of the words "rare" and "scarce."

120.   What is the Roman numeral for 3,000?

121.   What is the military time equivalent for 12:15 A.M.?

122.   What does MOBOT stand for?

123.   What is the initialism for "general intelligence"?

124.   What is the FLW?

125.   What does UNICEF stand for?

126.   Locate a list of synonyms for the word "necessary."

127.   What were the major world events of the 1450s?

128.   What does "logo" mean?

129.   Find synonyms and antonyms for the word "sweet."

130.   What is a "moonshiner"?

131.   Find an etymology of the word "shoe," with quotations showing its usage since 1150 A.D.

132.   What does ROCMM stand for?

133.    What does "modus vivendi" mean?

134.    Do "machine screw" and "machine steel" have the same
        initialism?

135.    Find a definition of the word "naskin," which was used
        in Great Britain in about 1670-1830.

136.    Was the phrase, "to lie in wait," used in the English
        language before 1620?

137.    What is the meaning of the phrase, "si fortuna juvat"?

138.    Find the German equivalents of "down and out" and
        "down-Easter."

139.    What is the Spanish equivalent of the verb "help"?

140.    Locate the etymology of the word "Geschichte."

141.    What is the etymology of the Spanish term "infanteria"?

142.    What does an Englishman mean when he speaks of his
        "hat covering his family"?

143.    Where can one find translations of the words referring
        to the parts of a camera?

144.    What do the abbreviations, "ss fx," "bldi," and "4R"
        stand for?

145.    Find a lengthy discussion with quotations on the mean-
        ings of the Spanish word "abreviar."

146.    What is a "ding-a-ling"?

147.    Find a historical summary of the meanings and uses
        of the German word "erarbeiten."

148.    What is the acronym for the solar energy research
        firm, Energy Conversion Devices?

149.    What is a "flutter wheel"?  When and by whom was it
        patented?

150.    What is the German word for "carfare"?

151. What is a "daftar"?

152. What does NATO stand for?

153. What is the Beecher's Bible?

154. What time of year is Adar?

155. How is the word "mesdames" pronounced?

156. How is the word "pekinese" spelled?

157. What is the Latin name for the swamp privet?

158. What is a "hillbilly"?

159. How long is a fathom?

160. Where was Ferdinand, King of Aragon, born?

161. What is a dandelion?

162. What is the current use of the word, "consensus"?

163. What is the meaning of the term, "hematogenesis"?

164. What does the word, "polar," mean?

165. Where is Shasta?

166. What does the word, "nudnick," mean?

167. What is Oxygen Point?

## Reference Materials

Abbreviations Dictionary
Acronyms, Initialisms and Abbreviations Dictionary
The American College Dictionary
American Heritage Dictionary of the English Language
Appleton's New Cuyas English-Spanish and Spanish-English
    Dictionary

Bernstein's Reverse Dictionary
Cassell's French Dictionary
Cassell's German Dictionary
Cassell's Spanish Dictionary
Children's World Book Dictionary
Deutsches Wörterbuch
Diccionario de la lengua española
Dictionnaire alphabétique et analogique de la langue française
A Dictionary of American English on Historical Principles
Dictionary of American Slang
A Dictionary of Americanisms
A Dictionary of Contemporary American Usage
Dictionary of Foreign Phrases and Abbreviations
Dictionary of Foreign Terms
Dictionary of Modern English Usage
A Dictionary of Slang and Unconventional English
Funk and Wagnalls New Standard Dictionary of the English
    Language
Funk and Wagnalls Standard College Dictionary
Harper Dictionary of Contemporary Usage
Harrap's New Standard French and English Dictionary
Langenscheidt's New Muret-Sanders Encyclopedic Dictionary
    of English and German Languages
Larousse Modern French-English (English-French) Dictionary
NBC Handbook of Pronunciations
Oxford English Dictionary
Random House Dictionary of the English Language
Reverse Acronyms, Initialisms and Abbreviations Dictionary
Roget's International Thesaurus
Roget's II: The New Thesaurus
Scott, Foresman Beginning Dictionary
Scott, Foresman Intermediate Dictionary
Thorndike-Barnhart Advanced Junior Dictionary
Webster's Collegiate Thesaurus
Webster's New Collegiate Dictionary
Webster's New World Dictionary
Webster's Third New International Dictionary of the English
    Language

# CHAPTER 7

## HANDBOOKS

### Reference Interviews

Patron #1.   A woman.

Patron:      I'm giving a Christmas party, and I want to know how to do it.
Librarian:   Do you mean that you want party plans, food recipes, plans for decorating--things like that?
Patron:      No, more what I should do: what's proper.
Librarian:   Do you mean how to be a hostess?
Patron:      Yes.

             Where would you find this information?


Patron #2.   A middle-aged woman.

Patron:      I'd like some information about eating.
Librarian:   What sort of information?
Patron:      Well, my daughter and I had an argument about asparagus. She said that you should eat it with your fingers and I said that was sloppy. So, I thought that you might have some sort of book that would tell me who was right.

             Where would you look?


Patron #3.   An elderly woman.

Patron:      Do you have any books about clubs?

Librarian: Yes, we do. What sort of book did you have
in mind? How to form a club, parliamentary
procedure, fund raising ideas, etc.?
Patron: I don't exactly know. I've just been elected
president of my church group, and I don't know
all those rules about bringing meetings to order,
passing motions, and things like that.

What would you suggest?


Patron #4. A high school girl.

Patron: Can you help me? We had a discussion in history
class today and I've been assigned to find out the
answer.
Librarian: What was the discussion about?
Patron: It was about the first American child. My teacher
said it was Virginia Dare, but some kids in my
class disagreed.
Librarian: What do you mean by American? Do you mean
the first child born in North America of European
parents or the first child born in an English
colony, or what?
Patron: I guess the first child born in America of parents
from any European country.

Where could you find the answer?


Patron #5. A elementary school teacher.

Patron: Do you have any books about Halloween?
Librarian: Do you want a collection of spooky stories and,
if so, for what reading level?
Patron: I don't want story books. I'm teaching a sixth
grade class this year, and I want to tell them
the history of Halloween and how it's celebrated
in other countries.

Where would you look?


Patron #6. A man.

Patron: I heard something on the radio a few weeks ago
about the largest check ever written on a bank.

I think it was paid to Sears, but I'm not sure.
It may have been Montgomery Ward or J. C.
Penney.   Anyway, could you find out some more
information about it for me?

Librarian:     How much information do you need?
Patron:        Oh, I'd like to know how much it was for and
               what bank it was written on and who it was paid
               to.

               Where is the answer?


Patron #7.     A high school boy.

Patron:        Do you have any dictionaries of history?
Librarian:     What was it you wanted to know--the meaning of
               some term?
Patron:        Not exactly.   I don't want to bother reading a
               whole long encyclopedia article or book on some-
               thing.   I just want to find a short synopsis.
Librarian:     Is this a historical period or event or person?
Patron:        The New Deal.

               Where could you find a brief synopsis?


## Reference Questions

1.  What is the origin of April Fool's Day?

2.  Who is the tallest woman in the world?

3.  Has any person ever lifted more than a ton?

4.  What university offered the first bibliography course?
    When?

5.  What gift is suggested as an alternative to the traditional
    bronze as a wedding anniversary gift?

6.  To what did "corduroy roads" refer in the period of
    American westward expansion?

7.  How did Candlemas Day get its name?

8. What is the proper size for a business card?

9. Is it possible to amend a resolution of censure by replacing the word "censure" with "thanks"?

10. Which baseball outfielder was called "Cherokee" and why?

11. What is "chronom-hoton-theolgos"?

12. Who was the 1928 Olympic discus champion and what was his throw?

13. When was the football dummy introduced to aid in teaching tackling?

14. What was the Ecbasis Captivi?

15. In what country did fencing as a sport originate?

16. Who made the first fire engine built in this country?

17. Which first lady was known as the "Bonny Brown Wife"?

18. Who introduced the fork in America?

19. Who was the "fraud President"?

20. What city is known as the Gibraltar of Louisiana?

21. Who was "the girl with the ginger-snap name"?

22. What is the opening line of a story in verse, published in the 19th century, about a goose which the cook sent to the table with only one leg?

23. What is Hognor Bread?

24. Who invented the ice-making machine of the vapor compression type?

25. Which firm of architects designed Iowa's state capitol building?

26. Which state is known as the Italy of America?

27. Who would use a "jesse" and what is it?

28. What are the names of the three Graces?

29. When Jennie Lind is lavender, blue, scarlet, and yellow, what is she?

30. Who was Kiddo?

31. What did the Know Ye Party advocate?

32. What was significant about the establishment of the Contra Costa Laundry in the U. S. in 1851?

33. When were American soldiers first granted free mailing privileges?

34. What day belonged to the Lord of Misrule?

35. What was the Mississippi Bubble?

36. Who wrote the words to Joseph R. Howard's Montana?

37. Who originated the idea of Mother's Day?

38. The motto of which American state is in Spanish?

39. What state is known as the Mud-Cat state?

40. What American President had a Newspaper Cabinet?

41. How long does it take to boil an ostrich egg?

42. When is Patriots' Day celebrated?

43. Pelota was introduced to early 16th-century Spain by Hernando Cortez as a "merry festival"; what is its American name or equivalent?

44. How is a pirouette executed in gymnastics?

45. Which variety of sunfish is known as a pumpkinseed?

46. In which world war did "Red One" fight?

47. What is the remotest island in the world and what are the two nearest land masses?

48. In what sport was Sad Sam famous?

49. Should a salad be eaten with a knife and fork, and was this always the custom?

50. Stalky, McTurk and Beetle were all based on real people; who are they?

51. How much should one tip?

52. What is the meaning of u. a. m. ? of magg. ?

53. How long should a widow wear mourning clothes?

54. What did the Wisconsin capitol cost?

55. Find an article on curling.

56. Where was the first watch repair shop in the U. S. located?

57. How did Indiana get its nickname?

58. Where can I find a list of world champion billiard players?

59. Where is the world's largest flag?

60. What was the year in which the first Thanksgiving Day was celebrated in America?

61. In what sport would one use a furnace dun?

62. What is a "drop" in reference to sports?

63. Where may I find advice on how to plan a formal dinner?

64. What was the name of the first university building in America?

65. Which saints are associated with October 22?

66. What is the state song of North Carolina?

67. To which famous couple do the English consecrate May Day?

68. Where can you find information which would help a stu-

dent of literature identify "Grishkin" and the "Brazilian Jaguar" in T. S. Eliot's "Whispers of Immortality"?

69. Where may I find the basic rules of football?

70. What is the meaning of "stirrup" in equitation and gymnastics?

71. Where could I find suggestions for appropriate gifts for shut-ins?

72. When was football first played in the United States?

73. By what name was Mary Todd called before her marriage to Abe Lincoln?

74. What is the correct table setting for the bridal party?

75. When was the first rebellion of Colonists against the English?

76. Should a young couple share the honeymoon cost?

77. When was Duncan Phyfe born, and what was his occupation?

78. Why is Ohio called the Buckeye state?

79. What "firsts" have occurred on April 28 in the U.S.?

80. What colors are permissible for a debutante's dress?

81. The world's largest overdue book fine was recorded a number of years ago. For how much was it, and how long had the book been due?

82. What appellations have been given James Knox Polk?

83. What are the correct dimensions of a playing court for lawn tennis?

84. What does the word "pole" mean?

85. Why is "Eureka" the motto of California?

86. When was the first American fire engine made?

87. Who and when does one tip while traveling on a luxury liner?

88. Who was the heaviest man ever to be weighed officially?

89. What city was given the name "Flower City"?

90. Who was the "Harness Horse of the Year" in 1947 (as selected by Nation's Turf Writers)?

91. What are the correct procedures for a military wedding?

92. Where could I find a bibliography of books about American patriotic holidays?

93. Which U. S. President coined the term "muckracker" and to what character does it refer?

94. Should the word "mister" be written in full or abbreviated on a wedding invitation?

95. Where is the world's largest castle located?

96. What is the world's gastronomic record for eating bananas?

97. Who holds the record for non-stop talking?

98. Find a brief biography of Eleanor of Aquitaine, Queen of Louis VII.

99. Locate a summary of The Odyssey.

100. Find an explanation of existentialism.

101. Identify Anna Karenina.

102. What are some of the "firsts" for Ann Arbor, Michigan?

103. What events happened on December 19, 1620?

104. Locate a bibliography of materials for information about the red legs of the Civil War.

105. What was "Seward's Folly"?

106.  Who was the Borax King?

107.  Which college athletes are known as the Lord Jeffs?

108.  What does one wear for an audience with the Pope?

109.  How does one write a bread-and-butter note?

110.  What is the proper attire for a formal evening wedding?

111.  What is the proper method of recessing a meeting?

112.  How does one second a motion?

113.  What is the correct form for the minutes of a meeting?

114.  What are the duties of a treasurer of an organization?

115.  What are the positions and numbers for a game of
      volleyball?

116.  Locate information about the history of archery.

117.  How does one run a round robin tournament?

118.  What is the proper manner for making an introduction
      at a party?

119.  Find a summary of King Lear.

120.  Locate a list of National League batting champions
      since 1901.

121.  Must you be recognized by the chair before seconding
      a motion?

122.  Where is the world's longest suspension bridge?

123.  Who made the first non-stop, cross-country airplane
      flight in the United States?

124.  How did the nickname "Hoosier" originate for the state
      of Indiana?

125.  How does one set the table for a small buffet?

126.  What are the rules for scoring a bowling game?

127. Who was the first astronaut in the United States?

128. What is the correct way to announce the arrival of a new baby?

129. Find a history of golf.

130. Identify the literary character, Raskolnikov.

131. What are the duties of a vice-president of an organization?

132. Who is the world's fattest man?

133. Who was the "Poet of the American Revolution"?

134. How does one use finger-bowls when dining?

135. How does one fill out a baseball box card?

136. Find a summary of the novel, Alice Adams, by Booth Tarkington.

137. What are several ways a parent can keep a child from smoking?

138. How did Idaho get its name?

139. Who was the first baseball pitcher to pitch a perfect no-hit, no-run, no-walk World Series game?

140. Locate a history of the Santa Fe Fiesta.

141. What is the tallest man-made structure in the world?

142. What is a "coffin corner" in football?

143. What is the "realistic" school of literature?

144. Did Albert Camus ever read R. L. Stevenson's Weir of Hermiston?

145. What is the proper form for addressing the Pope in conversation?

146. Should the treasurer's report be included in the secretary's minutes?

147. Should one say, "Lydia, this is Paul," or "Paul, this is Lydia"?

148. Who was "Old Gimlet Eye"?

149. Find a synopsis of Paradise Lost.

150. In what novel is Bill Sikes a character?

151. Find a history of field hockey in the United States.

152. Should an invitation to a wedding reception be acknowledged?

153. Who first used anesthesia?

154. Who originated Mother's Day?

155. Into what three states does Yellowstone National Park extend?

156. What goes in the constitution and by-laws of a club?

157. Where do the speaker and the president sit at a speaker's table?

158. How does one address the Assistant Secretary of the Interior?

159. Can a negative vote concerning a Parliamentary inquiry be reconsidered?

160. Who pays for various wedding expenses?

161. Where may one find advice on letters of condolence?

162. What store had the first escalator in the United States?

163. When a registered delegate of a convention wishes to end his or her presence, to what body must the departure be reported?

164. Find a synopsis of The Three Musketeers.

165. What is an appropriate gift for a fifteenth wedding anniversary?

166. What was the first school for higher education for women in the United States?

167. What are the major rules for pinochle?

168. When was the first time Franklin Delano Roosevelt appeared on television?

169. Who was Dulcinea del Toboso?

## Reference Materials

All About American Holidays
American Book of Days
American Nicknames
The Amy Vanderbilt Complete Book of Etiquette
Anniversaries and Holidays
Chases' Calendar of Annual Events
Dictionary of Phrase & Fable
The Dictionary of Sports
The Encyclopedia of Sports
Facts About the Presidents
Famous First Facts
Festivals Sourcebook
Guinness Book of World Records
The New Emily Post's Etiquette
Notes and Queries
The Reader's Encyclopedia
Robert's Rules of Order Newly Revised
Scarne's Encyclopedia of Games
State Names, Flags, Seals, Songs, Birds, Flowers and Other Symbols

# CHAPTER 8

## SERIAL PUBLICATIONS

### Reference Interviews

Patron #1.   A young boy.

| | |
|---|---|
| Patron: | Where can I find ... I'm doing a report on fishing, ship building, livestock, and ships.  I think that's all. |
| Librarian: | That's a lot.  Do you mean livestock like farm animals or are you talking about stocking water with fish? |
| Patron: | Farm animals. |
| Librarian: | Do you want books to take home? |
| Patron | If you have any.  All my material is supposed to be about recent developments in the last year. |

Where would you look first?

Patron #2.   A high school girl.

| | |
|---|---|
| Patron: | Where do you keep the books on black problems. I can't find anything in the card catalog. |
| Librarian: | Is it recent black problems that you have in mind? |
| Patron: | Yes.  It's for current events class. |
| Librarian: | Your best source for current events is magazines and newspapers. |
| Patron: | I have to know, too, how people reacted to the death of Martin Luther King. |

Where could you find this information?

Patron #3.    An older man.

Patron:       I'm investigating the Pueblo Incident.   I want
              to know what happened then.   You know, what
              the status of the whole affair is at present.
Librarian:    The Pueblo Incident was in January of 1968,
              wasn't it?
Patron:       Yes, that's right.

              Where would you look?


Patron #4.    A high school girl.

Patron:       I need some book reviews on Muhammed.
Librarian:    Is that the name of a book?
Patron:       Yes.
Librarian:    Do you know who the author is or when it was
              published?
Patron:       No.
Librarian:    Do you have the book with you?
Patron:       Yes.
Librarian:    We need to know the name of the author.   Here
              she is.   It's by Ruth Warren and this gives the
              year of publication.
Patron:       So where do I go now for reviews?

              Where could you find reviews?


Patron #5.    A man.

Patron:       I want to find out what has happened to Powell
              recently.
Librarian:    Do you mean Adam Clayton Powell?
Patron:       The former congressman.
Librarian:    How recently do you mean--in the last week or
              month?
Patron:       I need to know since the Supreme Court ruled
              the House of Representatives action unconstitu-
              tional.
Librarian     Do you know what date that was?
Patron:       No.

              Where would you check?


Patron #6.    A local general practitioner.

Patron:        I need some information on abortions.
Librarian:     Have you checked the card catalog and pamphlet
               file?
Patron:        Yes.   You don't have what I want.
Librarian:     Did you want something more recent?
Patron:        Yes.   I want to find out some of the international
               viewpoints on abortion.

               Where would you look?


Patron #7.     A woman.

Patron:        Has Anne Sexton died?
Librarian:     The poet?
Patron:        Yes, the American poet.
Librarian:     If she had died, it would have been recently?
Patron:        Yes.

               Where could you check?


Patron #8.     A high school boy.

Patron:        I'm doing the pro side of a debate on the grape
               boycott for my high school English class.   Where
               can I get some information?

               Where could you check?


Patron #9.     A high school girl.

Patron:        Do you have any information on Thor Heyerdahl,
               who wrote Kon Tiki?
Librarian:     There aren't any books on him as a writer.
Patron:        What I want are reviews of his writing.

               Where could you find reviews?


Patron #10.    A woman.

Patron:        I'm looking for a book on publishing.
Librarian:     What aspect of publishing did you have in mind?
Patron:        Oh, the names of different editors.
Librarian:     In the book industry?

Patron:        No, for magazines.
Librarian:     Did you have one magazine in mind?
Patron:        Yes, I wanted to know the editor of the maga-
               zine Human Events.

               Where could you find this information?


Patron #11. A girl.

Patron:        Does the library have issues of magazines from
               the 1930s?
Librarian:     Yes, we do--some of the more popular magazines,
               such as Time, Life, and Saturday Evening Post.
               Are you looking for a certain topic?
Patron:        Yes--discrimination against the American Indians
               in the 1930s, and what was happening to them at
               that time.

               Where would you look?


Patron #12. A high school boy.

Patron:        Do you have information on the Suez Canal?
Librarian:     What type of information?
Patron:        I want to find out what happened in the conflict
               there. Not what happened in the area of the
               canal but only the events that occurred right on
               the canal itself--the dates it opened and closed.

               Where would you look for detailed information?


Patron #13. A young woman.

Patron:        Do you have any recent articles on swapping
               wives?

               Where would you look?


Patron #14. A woman.

Patron:        I would like to get some information about the
               Bataan Death March.
Librarian:     What kind of information do you need?

Patron:     I just found out that my father-in-law was one
            of the prisoners, and I would like to read some
            magazine articles about what happened.

            Where would you find periodical articles?


## Reference Questions

1.  How much of the series, Masters in Art, is owned by
    Allegheny College?

2.  Does any American library have a complete file of the
    Arkhiv of the Institut Marksa-Engelsa-Lenina?

3.  What are the names of the principal college newspapers
    In Illinois?

4.  Who wrote an article on the "Art of Plagiarism" which
    appeared in a magazine in 1904?

5.  Where can you find information on the early files of the
    newspaper, The Boston Recorder?

6.  Locate libraries in the U.S. that have files of the China
    Journal. Do any Canadian libraries have it?

7.  In what magazine did George Meredith's Diana of the
    Crossways appear in the 1880s?

8.  Can you locate periodical articles about the Dreyfus af-
    fair that were written at the time of the event?

9.  Can you find a review of Jane Eyre by Charlotte Brontë,
    by one of her contemporaries?

10. Did Zechariah Fowle have anything to do with the Exeter
    (New Hampshire) Journal in 1778-1779?

11. Locate E. A. Freeman's review of Grote's History of
    Greece, written in the middle of the nineteenth century.

12. In what libraries can the publications of the K. Freie
    ökonomische Gesellschaft zu St. Petersburg be found?

13. Which serial does Quarterly Demographic Bulletin, which began publication in 1979, continue?

14. Who wrote the article, "On the Trail of Geronimo," in the 1880s?

15. What is the oldest newspaper in Lexington, Massachusetts? Is there a complete file of it?

16. What is the circulation of the Lincoln (Nebraska) Journal?

17. How much of the series, Masters in Music, does the Nashville Public Library possess?

18. What is the aggregate circulation of all morning and evening newspapers in the U.S.?

19. Find a list of Latin American newspapers.

20. Does the Journal of the American Oil Chemists Society have abstracts or book reviews?

21. Locate current articles in American periodicals on the televising of sports.

22. Where did Thomas Hardy's Two on a Tower appear in the 1890s?

23. Where did George DuMaurier's Trilby appear in the 1890s?

24. Who is the editor of the London (England) Daily Express?

25. Who is the fashion editor of the Lafayette (Indiana) Journal and Courier?

26. I need a copy of the Lafayette Evening Call, a newspaper published in Lafayette, Indiana from 1883-1905. Where can I find it?

27. What is the circulation of the Montreal newspaper, La Presse?

28. Find a chronological index to news stories about Spanish politics and government which appeared last year.

29. Do any libraries in the U.S. have a copy of Volume

Three of Semaine des enfants, a French serial publication?

30. Locate news articles about Walt Disney's illness and death in 1966.

31. How often does Who's Who in the Midwest appear?

32. Are there any magazines on camping published in California?

33. What are the names and addresses of some manufacturers and suppliers of rotary presses used by newspapers?

34. Does the Illinois State Library have complete holdings of the Japanese Journal of Botany from 1922 to 1949?

35. How often is the Clinical Reporter, a serial which began in 1962, published?

36. In what languages is the magazine, Mines, available?

37. Where is Sports Illustrated indexed?

38. I would like a list, with short summaries, of recent newspaper articles on NATO.

39. Find a list of periodicals on the subject of international trade.

40. Find statistics about newspaper publishing in New York state.

41. Find a list of American libraries which have copies of the annual report of the Shanghai Meteorological Society.

42. Locate a historical sketch, as well as library holdings, of the newspaper, The Massachusetts Spy, from 1775 to 1820.

43. Who publishes Bibliothèque, the journal of the Ecole des Chartes? What is its price?

44. What periodical deals with traffic management?

45. Who is the editor of Canadian Swine?

46. Jackie Robinson was admitted to major league baseball in 1945. Where can I find newspaper accounts about this event and about racial discrimination in organized baseball during that year?

47. Where can I find an article on the canal system of Canada written in the nineteenth century?

48. I want to find the initial reactions of reviewers to Margaret Mitchell's Gone With the Wind. Where can I locate some of those old reviews?

49. Where can I find a review of Children of the Night by E. A. Robinson?

50. Where can I find newspaper articles which appeared immediately after the death of Amelia Earhart in 1937?

51. Where can I find an article on the career of King Edward VII of England?

52. William Manchester's Death of a President received mixed reactions from the press. Where can I find the pro and con reactions by the reviewers?

53. How can I locate a text of U Thant's address to the convocation of Pacem in Terris II?

54. How can I find an article on French feelings toward Germany in 1891?

55. Where can I find an article about George Keats, brother of the poet, written during his lifetime?

56. How did the New York Times report the political viewpoints and activities of Representative Martin Dies, Chairman of the House Committee investigating un-American activities in the late 1930s?

57. In conjunction with research on the development of advertising during the years from 1895 to 1910, I need to examine newspapers from that era. I prefer to do the research in the Philadelphia area. What nearby institutions have newspaper files for this period?

58. Where can I find an article by G. T. Winston about high education in the South in 1897?

59.  Where can one locate a criticism of the movie, "Bus Stop," when it originally appeared?

60.  I need to know the years when John Fenno printed the Gazette of the United States.

61.  Is there a complete run of the Spectator in the United States?

62.  I would like to know the subscription price to libraries and the circulation of Chemical Abstracts.

63.  Are there any Estonian publications in Canada?

64.  Where could one find articles about ophthalmology indexed?

65.  Are there any play review indexes?

66.  What subjects does The Topicator Index cover?

67.  Locate a periodical article about fireproof construction printed before 1881.

68.  Locate a 1929 article about abolishing Sunday.

69.  Where would one find a list of reviews of last year's television programs?

70.  In which periodical index could one find references to articles about quadraphonic sound systems?

71.  Locate a reference in a popular magazine about economic conditions in Japan.

72.  Where would one find a list of periodical indexes in the field of anthropology?

73.  In which periodical did an article by Henry James entitled "Daumier, the Caricaturist" appear in the late nineteenth century?

74.  Locate a list of daily newspapers published in Massachusetts.

75.  Find a list of serial publications about brides.

76. Locate the name of a Chinese daily newspaper published in Vancouver, B. C.

77. Does the New York Times accept mail order advertising?

78. Who is the manager of the circulation department of the Milwaukee Journal?

79. Find a list of current periodicals concerned with native Americans.

80. Does The Journal of Social Sciences have book reviews?

81. What is the circulation of the Hawaii AFL-CIO News?

82. Where is The British Journal of Radiology indexed?

83. When did The Atlantic Magazine begin publication?

84. What is the price of The Japan Economic Year Book?

85. What are the advertising rates of The Valley News, a Lebanon, New Hampshire newspaper?

86. How much does a subscription to Time cost?

87. Which Canadian libraries receive Norois, a French geographic magazine which began publication in 1954?

88. What are the names of current periodicals published about the grocery trade?

89. When was Whitaker's Almanack founded?

90. Find a list of periodicals concerning the hotel industry.

91. Find a citation to a news article about funeral plans for John Steinbeck.

92. Locate a list of magazine articles about Benjamin Disraeli published during the nineteenth century.

93. How often is Theoretical Chemical Engineering Abstracts, which began publication in 1964, issued?

94. Who publishes the serial, Rio Grande do Sul?

95. Who are the chief editors of the Fairfield, Iowa Ledger, a daily newspaper?

96. Does The YWCA Magazine contain book reviews?

97. What is the address of the publishers of the Frozen Foods Year Book?

98. What are the titles of some indexes which have reviews of recent motion pictures?

99. Who has copies of the Los Angeles Times for 1900?

100. Locate periodical articles about sports on television.

101. What types of articles are included in The Antique Dealer, a periodical?

102. Locate a reference to an obituary of Virgil Grissom, the astronaut from the United States.

103. Which newspapers did William A. Davis print between 1802-1803?

104. What is the price for a subscription to Banker's Magazine?

105. Find a list of libraries which have copies of Crawdaddy, a musical periodical which began publication in 1966.

106. What libraries have copies of the 1817 editions of the Detroit Gazette?

107. Find references to periodical articles about the economic conditions in Europe which were published between 1870 and 1880.

108. In which work would be found a reference to a periodical article on factory management written in the second decade of the nineteenth century?

109. Does the University of Maine Library receive copies of the periodical, Human Relations News of Chicago, which came out in 1959?

110. What magazine superseded the Intellectual Observer, which ceased publication in 1868?

111. Does any library have a copy of the January 20, 1838 issue of the Chicago American, a newspaper?

112. Find a list, with short summaries, of recent newspaper articles on NATO.

113. How much does the Year Book of Obstetrics and Gynecology cost?

114. What libraries have copies of the periodical, Doctor's Wife, published between 1960 and 1962?

115. Which libraries have copies of a magazine called Shipmate, which began in 1938?

116. Locate information on the Pennsylvania Gazette, a newspaper published between 1728 and 1815.

117. Find a description of Science Citation Index and the type of book reviews it contains.

118. What library has copies of the periodical, Shoe and Leather Facts, which was published from 1889 to 1938?

119. What is the circulation for the Chicago Tribune?

120. In what libraries could one find the American Association of School Librarians' Newsletter, which began publication in 1951?

121. What is the address of the publisher of the Catholic Library Association's Directory?

122. Who publishes the National Flaxseed Processors Yearbook?

123. Who publishes the Pottery Quarterly?

124. Locate periodical articles on Israel for a high school term paper.

125. Locate periodical articles on the Middle East for a club's program.

126. Find periodical articles on employment of the handicapped.

127.    Locate periodical articles on ceramics.

128.    Locate periodical articles on the family.

129.    Find periodical articles on conditions in France.

130.    Locate periodical articles on problems of young people.

131.    Locate periodical articles about the conditions of Navaho
        Indians.

132.    Find references to articles on present-day employment
        compared with that of the past.

133.    Find periodical articles on planning a family budget.

134.    Locate references to reviews of plays on Broadway.

135.    Find periodical articles on the Depression of the 1930s.

136.    Find periodical articles on women in industry.

137.    Find periodical articles on the political situation in
        Italy.

138.    Find periodical articles on the accomplishments of the
        United Nations during the past year.

139.    What are some of the pros and cons of euthanasia?

140.    Find a list of periodical articles on cybernetics.

141.    Find a list of recent periodical articles on heart di-
        sease.

142.    Find periodical articles on socialized medicine.

143.    Find book reviews of The Big Fisherman.

144.    Locate periodical articles about UNESCO.

145.    Find periodical articles on spastic children.

146.    Locate periodical articles for a high school paper on
        genocide.

147.    Locate periodical articles for a paper on communism.

148. Locate periodical articles about the effects of nicotine on the heart.

149. Find magazine articles on the status of women in the USSR.

150. Find periodical articles on recent labor legislation.

151. Locate reviews of O'Hara's Rage to Live.

152. Find materials for a paper on "Alaska Today."

153. Locate materials for a speech on Americanism.

154. Locate materials on some of the latest progress in the field of medicine.

155. Find materials for a paper on the countries of southwest Asia.

156. Find a list of periodical articles on how to reduce fat on the hips and the waist.

157. Who publishes the Alaskan Sportsman?

158. What are the addresses of some ophthalmic publications?

159. What is the leading newspaper in Sioux City, Iowa?

160. Find reviews of The Cocktail Party by T. S. Eliot.

161. Find a review of Maria Theresa by Bright, published in 1897.

162. What are some of the titles published in the monograph series of the Community Mental Health Journal?

163. Find the address of the publisher of Musical America.

164. Where is the magazine Hardware Retailer published?

165. What is the abbreviation for the American Journal of Nursing?

166. What is the address of the Argus Publishers Corporation?

167. Locate a list of periodical articles about collegiate basketball.

168. What did S. J. Gould publish in 1981?

169. Find references to recent newspaper articles about protests by university students in France.

## Reference Materials

Access
American Newspapers, 1821-1936
Ayer Directory of Publications
Book Review Digest
Book Review Index
Books in Series
Children's Book Review Index
Current Book Review Citations
History and Bibliography of American Newspapers, 1690-1820
International Index to Multi-Media Information
International Yearbook
Internationale Bibliographie der Zeitschriftenliteratur aus allen Gebieten des Wissens
Irregular Serials and Annuals
Magazine Index
Magazine Industry Market Place
Media Review Digest
New Periodicals Index
New Serial Titles
New York Times Index
New York Times Obituaries Index
Newspaper Indexes
Periodical Title Abbreviations
Poole's Index to Periodical Literature
Popular Periodical Index
Readers' Guide to Periodical Literature
Sources of Serials
Standard Periodical Directory
Titles in Series
Ulrich's International Periodicals Directory
Union List of Serials in Libraries of the United States and Canada
Women's Studies Abstracts

CHAPTER 9


DIRECTORIES


## Reference Interviews


Patron #1.  A high school teacher.

Patron        I would like some information on SIECUS.
Librarian:    Do you know what those letters stand for?
Patron:       Not exactly.  It has something to do with sex.
Librarian:    First I'll have to look up the meaning of the
              letters.  (Found in DeSola, Abbreviations Dic-
              tionary.)  It means Sex Information and Education
              Council of the United States.

              Where would you go for further information?


## Reference Questions


1. Where is the headquarters of the eastern region of the
   Postal Inspection Service?

2. What railroads serve Romeo, Illinois?

3. Which state carries the numerical prefixes 750-799 for
   its zip code?

4. What are some of the activities of the Huguenot Historical Society in the U.S.?

5. What products does the Jeffrey Manufacturing Division of Dresser Industries make?

6. Does the Holiday Inn in Marietta, Georgia have a swimming pool?

7. Which credit cards will Eastern Airlines accept?

8. Where would you look to find out if your neighbor owns his or her home or is renting it?

9. What are the visa regulations for U. S. citizens travelling in Egypt? Are any inoculations required?

10. Find the address of the Zinc Institute and the name of its chief executive officer.

11. How many professors are on the Faculty of Theology at Oxford?

12. What airlines serve Tulsa, Oklahoma?

13. Where could you find the address of the British Council in Jordan?

14. What are the major libraries of Costa Rica?

15. Where would you look to determine what resort establishments the American Hotel and Motel Association sponsors in Bermuda?

16. What is the name of an airport near Pisa, Italy and which airlines use its facilities?

17. Does the Hyatt Islandia in San Diego, California have the facilities to accommodate a convention of 1,000 participants at any time of the year?

18. Which manufacturer of screw machine products in Lancaster, Pennsylvania has the most tangible assets?

19. Where can I find a list of money and exchange rates that is up to date for this month?

20. When was the University of Cairo founded?

21. What is the airline mileage between New York and San Francisco?

22. Where can I locate a list of the manufacturers of steel abrasives?

23. Are there any organizations in New Jersey which focus on ethnic folklore?

24. What are the hours of the Metropolitan Museum of Art?

25. Find a list of motels near Manchester, Ohio.

26. Where should I look to discover what national, nonprofit associations are centered in Arkansas?

27. Can you find a list of historical societies in the U.S.?

28. When and where is the annual convention of the Sigmund Freud archives usually held?

29. What is the name of an international student relief organization and what activities does it sponsor?

30. Who is the manager of the Statler Hilton in Boston?

31. Find a list of dealers in foreign books.

32. What are the special book interests of The Blue Horn Book Shop in Smyrna, Delaware?

33. Who are the editors of Stackpole Book Publishing Company?

34. Find a list of media available from Gaylord Bros., Inc.

35. What is the address of the National Audio Visual Center in Washington, D.C.?

36. Find a list of book clubs in the United States.

37. Locate a calendar of media events and sponsors for the year.

38. What is the name of the general sales manager for WABC-AM radio station?

39. What is the telephone number of the Pennsylvania College of Optometry?

40. Does the Canadian Psychological Association have any publications?

41. Locate a list of universities and colleges in the Mongolian People's Republic.

42. When was Mu Phi Epsilon founded?   Name some of its committees and publications.

43. When was the Rockefeller Family Fund incorporated?

44. Who was the donor of the Coleman Charitable Trust located in Kansas?

45. What is the purpose of the Metropolitan Foundation of Atlanta, Georgia?

46. Where is the Starr Foundation located?

47. Locate financial data about the Merrill Foundation.

48. Where is the National Cash Register Foundation located and what are its functions?

49. Does the National Library of New Zealand include a library school?

50. Of what do the holdings of the Statistical Reporting Service of the United States government consist?

51. What associations are headquartered in Dearborn, Michigan?

52. How many local chapters does the Federal Bar Association have?

53. Where is the American Antiquarian Society located?

54. What is the name of the director of the Art Gallery of Hamilton, Ontario?

55. What are the special collections in the George F. Harding Museum in Chicago?

56. Does Sikkim have a university?

57. What is the address of the Lingerie Manufacturers Association?

58. What is the zip code of Bettendorf, Iowa?

59. When was Hiroshima University founded and how many students now attend classes?

60. Locate a list of museums in Moscow.

61. Locate a list of the members of the United States National Academy of Sciences.

62. What language is used for instruction at the University of Bombay, India?

63. What are the main subject collections of the Ghana National Museum?

64. Does Acheson Colloids Corporation solicit overseas trade?

65. What is the capital rating of the Western Supplies Company?

66. Where are the branch offices of the Allis-Chalmers Manufacturing Company located?

67. Who is the governing authority of the Historic Pensacola Preservation Board, located in Florida?

68. Who uses the Pensco trademark?

69. What are the locations of the Sheraton Hotels and Motels?

70. Has the Iolani Palace in Honolulu been designated an historic site?

71. How much does a room with twin beds cost per night in the Americana Hotel in New York?

72. Locate a list of U. S. libraries which house collections of special non-book materials.

73. How many wax museums are there in the U. S. and where are they located?

74. Which credit cards will Japan Air Lines accept?

75. Which airlines fly between Boston, Massachusetts and Albany, New York?

76. How much does it cost to fly on Delta Air Lines from Chicago to Caracas, Venezuela?

77. Find a map showing the routes flown by Mexicana Airlines.

78. What is the Pan Am airfare between New York and London?

79. Which factories in Michigan manufacture hydraulic couplings?

80. What is the airline fare between Detroit and Acapulco?

81. With which institution is the Museo de Arte Religioso, located in San German, Puerto Rico, affiliated?

82. What is the address of the American Theological Library Association?

83. Where is the Germantown Historical Society located?

84. What is the address of The Bookbinder's Guild of New York?

85. Does Braniff International Airlines fly to Mexico City from New York?

86. What are some of the publications of the Arkansas Agricultural Experiment Station?

87. Who is the director of the Tennessee State Museum?

88. What special printing services does Musigraph, Inc. offer?

89. Does Rizzoli International Publications, Inc. , located in New York, have any subsidiaries?

90. Does anyone make fluorescent light fixtures in Boston?

91. Find a list of literary contests.

92. Find a list of museums in London.

93. Does Paradise, Pennsylvania have its own post office?

94.  Find a list of academies and learned societies, with descriptions, arranged by country.

95.  Find a list of book publishers who specialize in atlases and maps.

96.  Are there any organizations in the U.S. which translate works written in Tagalog?

97.  Locate a list of Avis and Hertz car rental agencies.

98.  What is the name of a large manufacturer of greeting cards which is located in Cleveland.

99.  What are the activities of the Federal Deposit Insurance Corporation?

100.  Is there a post office in Moody, Texas?

101.  In what state is the Acadia National Park Bookstore located?

102.  Locate information on the Society for the Prevention of Cruelty to Animals.

103.  What are the hours when the Mark Twain Museum in Hannibal, Missouri is open to the public?

104.  What is the purpose of the National Council of Teachers of Mathematics?

105.  What kinds of materials does the Pooh Corner Book and Record Shop in Denver stock?

106.  When was the Stevens Institute of Technology in Hoboken, New Jersey founded?

107.  What is the address of the company which produces Timex watches?

108.  What type of works make up the holdings of the National Science Foundation Library in Washington?

109.  Is Allis Chalmers connected with General Motors?

110.  What is the address of a company from which a patron may purchase silicone?

111.  Where is the headquarters of the Cokesbury Book Shop
      in Syracuse, New York located?

112.  What is the address of the White Sewing Machine Com-
      pany?

113.  The Rockwood Museum Shop in Wilmington, Delaware
      specializes in books on which subjects?

114.  What is the address of the Benjamin Electrical Com-
      pany?

115.  What firms manufacture rubber suction cups?

116.  Does the B. Dalton Bookseller chain have a branch
      store in Fargo, North Dakota?

117.  What is the address of the Corning Glass Company?

118.  What is the zip code for the U.S. military base in
      Reggio Calambria, Italy?

119.  What is the address of the U.S. office of the World
      Union of Jewish Students?

120.  Find the title of a video recording about the life cycle
      of the silk moth.

121.  Find the titles of a film dealing with teenage sexuality.

122.  What are the titles of some filmstrips available on
      black studies?

123.  What information can be found in the ADELE data bases?

124.  At which universities is research being done on music
      therapy?

125.  To which publishers is the ISBN 0-8143 assigned?

126.  What is the telephone number of the National Associa-
      tion of Chewing Gum Manufacturers?

127.  Where is Robert Cohen, a mathematician, employed?

128.  Locate data on information brokers in Colorado.

129.  Locate at least one title of a periodical for a reader
      interested in publishing an article on game theory.

130.  Find the title of a directory for municipal officials in
      Kansas.

131.  What is the correct name for the Better Business
      Bureau for the Miami area?


## Reference Materials


American Book Trade Directory
Audio Visual Market Place
City Directories
Consumer Protection Directory
Directory of Directories
Directory of Online Databases
Directory of Post Offices
Directory of Publishing Opportunities
Educational Film Locator of the Consortium of University
    Film Centers
Encyclopedia of Associations
The Foundation Directory
Hotel and Motel Red Book
Information Industry Market Place
Information Resources of the U. S. Government
The Literary Market Place
National Faculty Directory
National Information Center for Educational Media
National Trade and Professional Associations of the United
    States
Official Airline Guide
Official Guide of the Railways
Official Museum Directory
Publishers' International Directory
Research Centers Directory
Subject Guide to Periodical Indexes and Review Indexes
Thomas' Register of American Manufacturers
The Video Source Book
World of Learning
Yearbook of International Organizations
Zip Code Directory

# CHAPTER 10

## GOVERNMENT PUBLICATIONS

### Reference Interviews

<u>Patron #1</u>.    A high school student.

| | |
|---|---|
| Patron: | I need information on James Russell Grover. |
| Librarian: | Is he living, and what is his occupation? |
| Patron: | He has been a congressman from the State of New York. |
| Librarian: | In the U. S. House of Representatives? |
| Patron: | Yes. |

Where could you find this information?

<u>Patron #2</u>.    A woman.

| | |
|---|---|
| Patron: | What is the most recent address of the Social Security Office? |
| Librarian: | The main office in Baltimore or a more local one? |
| Patron: | The one in Baltimore. |

Where would you look?

### Reference Questions

1.    Is the journal of Rudolph F. Kurz to be found in the

Congressional Edition?  Where was it originally published in 1937?

2.  Who is the congressman for the fifth district of Minnesota in the present Congress?

3.  An article by Rex Beach titled "Modern Miracle Men" was published in the Congressional Set in 1936.  Where had it been previously printed?

4.  Who are the senators and representatives from Oklahoma?

5.  Where can one find a list of subjects covered in the Subject Bibliographies of government publications?

6.  Which congresspeople are on the Rules Committee?

7.  How can one locate Woodrow Wilson's "Proclamation of Existence of War with the German Empire"?

8.  I want a list of the public documents of the seventy-sixth Congress (1939-40) regarding natural resources.

9.  Who is the Chief of Naval Operations?

10.  Where would I find a list of publications by the Public Health Service in December of last year?

11.  What publications can be ordered from the U. S. Superintendent of Documents about the pulp and paper industry?

12.  Find the remarks made in the House of Representatives by Philip J. Philbin, Representative from Massachusetts on Wednesday, September 23, 1970.

13.  Locate the titles of several publications issued by NASA's Office of University Affairs in 1977.

14.  Where can an 1882 government report be found on the effects of Canadian and American tariffs?

15.  Who are the members of the House of Representatives Ways and Means Committee?

16.  What is "senatorial courtesy"?

17. In what congressional district is Enid, Oklahoma?

18. Where can one find recent listings of the Fish and Wild-life Service's publications?

19. A special report on the ship industry of the U.S. was written in 1892. It appeared in which government document, and who wrote it?

20. What report did William E. Paulson write for the U.S. government in 1939?

21. Find a list of the publications of the National Bureau of Standards for July of last year.

22. Where can I find a map of the Capitol building in Washington, D.C.?

23. What material was available from the Department of Agriculture on truck gardening in 1939?

24. Where would you go to compile a list of the publications of the State of Indiana received at the Library of Congress last year?

25. Where could I find a description of the activities of the Department of Commerce?

26. What newspapers are represented in the press galleries of the Congress?

27. Were there any government publications on defense proceedings in 1917?

28. Where could I find a list of the cabinet members under William McKinley?

29. Where could I find a list of the delegates to the Continental Congress?

30. Where can I find the voting statistics from the last Congressional election?

31. Who is the Postmaster General?

32. Find a list of government publications about railroad employees.

33. Find a description of how a bill becomes a law.

34. Locate brief descriptions of the legislative histories of public laws enacted last year.

35. What are the publications of the House Ways and Means Committee?

36. Locate histories of bills concerning the spillage of oil on the United States coastlines.

37. What bills has your congressperson introduced during the past year?

38. Find the text of the latest debates in the Congress on bills concerning water pollution.

39. Locate the texts of the President's addresses to the Congress for last year.

40. Find a list of special publications by the House and Senate.

41. What are the contents of the Madison Papers?

42. Who wrote the report on the Piute Indians which was published in 1872?

43. On what date was W. H. Scribner awarded a disability pension by Congress for injuries received in the Civil War?

44. Who was the Senate Republican Conference Chairman of the 97th Congress?

45. What is meant by a "clean bill"?

46. Who wrote a United States government report in 1883 about the financial and agricultural condition of Cuba?

47. What topics did President George Washington discuss in his annual message to Congress in 1790?

48. In which volume for a given session of Congress is Senate Report #792 located?

49. Which house documents are included in Volume 16 of the second session of the 84th Congress?

50. Locate a list of recent state publications on art exhibitions.

51. Does the Department of the Interior's Bureau of Outdoor Recreation still exist?

52. What publications has the Library of Congress received recently from the Department of Education in Georgia?

53. Which title of the Code of Federal Regulations deals with the Census Bureau?

54. Find an organizational breakdown of the Treasury Department in chart form.

55. What became of the War Assets Administration?

56. Who were the cabinet members during Franklin D. Roosevelt's third term?

57. Find a list of the Representatives from Tennessee for the 18th Congress.

58. Locate a list of Senate committees and their members.

59. In what congressional district is Washtenaw County, Michigan?

60. How is the Smithsonian Institution organized?

61. In what United States government document may one find a bibliography on the Eskimo language published in 1887?

62. What did the United States Children's Bureau publish in 1922?

63. Where can one find a brief abstract of a United States government report about the construction of a lighthouse at Thunder Bay, Michigan, in 1878?

64. When was the Sixteenth Ammendment of the U.S. Constitution ratified and what topic does it address?

65. Find a biography of Spencer Oliver Fisher, a Representative from Michigan from 1885 to 1889.

66. What is the mailing address for the United States Department of Defense?

67. What is the best source for titles of United States government publications on Israel for last year?

68. Find a reference to an 1892 government report on trade relations with Mexico.

69. Find the names of the present officers of the United States Senate.

70. Which government agency compiled a deficiency estimate for the U. S. Geological Survey for 1892-1893?

71. Did the United States government publish anything on the subject of antigens and antibodies in 1939?

72. What is the serial number of the recommendation concerning the Michigan and Mississippi River Canal introduced into the House of Representatives in 1884?

73. Which radio and television correspondents are admitted to the United States Congressional galleries?

74. Find the name of an official report on the exploration of the Yukon River in the Alaska Territory published by the United States government in April 1871.

75. Who wrote a government report on the payment of French officers of the American Revolution published on January 22, 1784?

76. Find a brief biography of Rose Long, a United States Senator in the 1930s.

77. What is the House Document No. 381 of the 87th Congress, 2nd Session?

78. Who is the United States Representative for the third district of this state?

79. Are there more lawyers than representatives of any other profession in Congress?

80. What is the address of a Senator from New Jersey?

81. Who is the chair of the National Endowment for the Humanities?

82.  Find a history of the Interstate Commerce Commission.

83.  Who is the United States Ambassador to the USSR?

84.  What is the formal title of the Warren Commission report?

85.  What are some of the major publications available for sale from the U. S. Government on the subject of agriculture?

## Reference Materials

Biographical Directory of the American Congress
Catalogue of the Public Documents of Congress and of All Departments of the Government of the U. S.
Comprehensive Index to the Publications of the U. S. Government, 1881-1893
Congressional Information Service Index to Publications of the U. S. Congress
Congressional Quarterly
Congressional Record
Descriptive Catalogue of the Government Publications of the U. S. (1774-1881)
Guide to U. S. Government Publications
Monthly Catalog of U. S. Government Publications
Monthly Checklist of State Publications
Numerical Lists and Schedule of Volumes
Official Congressional Directory
Subject Bibliographies
U. S. Government Manual